Parsley is World Peace in Disguise

ENJOY!

CHEF DER

ISBN: 1548888826
ISBN-13: 978-1548888824

Cover design by Tracey Jamieson

Dedicated to the loving memory of

Caryn Zimmerman

~

One of the most spirited & dynamic women ever.

I am proud to say she was my colleague,

but more importantly, my friend.

CONTENTS

Acknowledgements

Writing a book is a huge undertaking. Especially when one still must find the time to allocate to being a husband, father, and earning an income to contribute to the household. The thoughts of mine that have been transferred to paper, which you are holding, are a compilation that has taken a number of years to bring together. I first had the idea to write this specific book after I did a presentation for a local chamber of commerce group. I was doing a demonstration on the importance of garnishing when the words "parsley is world peace is disguise" randomly came to mind. One of the attendees approached me afterwards and said "That's quite a statement, but I understand exactly what you mean."

From that moment years ago, I've had that in mind as a book title and have been jotting down notes and ideas for this project ever since. Having my thoughts consumed about this book for so many years, must have driven my wife Katherine crazy. Thus she is the first I want to thank. Katherine is not only my partner in life and love, but she is also my best friend and soulmate. Time and time again, she has supported me through all my wild ideas and ventures. During times when projects like this consume me, she has been the parent in my absence, the leader of the household, and the foundation of our family. As an added bonus, she happens to be an English Major and has stepped up to plate as my own personal live-in Editor. Thank you so much Sweetheart for your unwavering love and devotion. You are the most incredible woman I have ever known and this book would have never come to life without you.

I want to also thank my four children for their patience and understanding. Again, the development of this book has kept me occupied away from you, many more times than I would have liked. Watching you grow, experience life, and conquering challenges makes me see the value of being a good parent, but it also makes me strive to be a better person as well. For all the times I was "too busy", and when I said "not now", I am truly sorry.

Although through your actions I know you understand, I still feel the need to make sure I tell you that without you, my life would not be complete. The joy of fatherhood has been more rewarding than any business endeavor I have ever embarked upon. Thank you so much for bringing so much meaning and purpose to my life.

Caryn Zimmerman, to whom this book is dedicated, deserves special recognition as well. Caryn was my friend, travel consultant and an integral part of the Chef Dez Culinary Tours. Although I had known Caryn for many years prior, she brought tremendous success to these tours in the years of 2014, 2015, and 2016. Her energetic and vibrant personality complimented my passion for people and food, and made us a perfect team for our tour guests time and time again. Unfortunately, Caryn passed away on June 27, 2017 from a fierce, but brief, battle with cancer. Caryn was always so full of life and she had a knack for bringing vitality to any party or function. We first met at one of my live cooking shows, and she was a huge supporter for me ever since. She consistently told me how much she believed in me, and her actions in all the events we did together proved it. Thank you for everything you did for me Caryn. You were such an important part of not only my career, but my life as well, and I miss you terribly. Rest in peace.

It was also because of Caryn, that I was able to meet Chef Michael Smith, who has graciously written the foreword of this book. The last culinary tour that Caryn and I hosted was to the Canadian province of Prince Edward Island in 2016, and the pinnacle of that trip was Michael's Inn at Bay Fortune. I have followed Chef Michael Smith's TV career from day one, and thus he has helped shaped my career into what it is today. In person, he is just as kind and welcoming as he appears on screen. Thank you Michael for the impact you have made on the culinary scene, and for your kindness and hospitable nature. I am honoured to have you write the foreword of this book.

I would also like to thank my sister-in-law Tracey Jamieson for the cover design of this book. Tracey, a graphic design artist by trade, is artistically talented in so many ways and I am thrilled to have her represent the primary focus of this project. Thank you for your generosity and for sharing your flair.

Thanks to my parents for their lifelong support and encouragement; to my best friend Dave who I have bounced ideas off of since grade four; and to all my family, friends, and acquaintances in my life that make it so complete.

Last, but definitely not least, I want to thank everyone who has attended my classes, welcomed me into their homes & businesses, attended my cooking shows, bought my books, travelled with me, and been a dedicated reader of my columns. Without you... none of this would be a reality. Thank you all so much.

Foreword

Food is trendy. It's center stage but while we seem to have more food than ever before less of us are cooks. Most of us are outsourcing. We eat out regularly and at home factories do much of the work. Processed food has not just dramatically eroded our health but also obliterated our true connection to food.

Chef Dez knows the way forward is through the kitchen. Only here can you find the quiet confidence to take charge of your food lifestyle. Embrace the path, for you and your family. Three simple steps. Gather. Prepare. Share.

Don't worry. You can do it. Don't confuse the unknown with impossible. It's in you. We've always cooked. Since fire was born. It's in us: an innate desire to come together around the table, around food. The social context of food is as important as what you eat. Who's at the table matters as much as what's on the table.

Food can fuel your authentic core well beyond your basic nutritional needs. Cooking for your family and friends can be regular and routine but it can also allow your spirit to soar to richly fulfilling heights. Time spent gathering, preparing, and sharing fills you with purpose through helping others. Each step of the way offers so much creative and gracious possibility. The first step may be the hardest but once you get started you'll find your path easily. And bring some parsley. You never know when it might come in handy!

Chef Michael Smith

Introduction

It was a cold afternoon in January 2003. I had just completed teaching my very first cooking class and I couldn't stop smiling. Sitting in my Chef's jacket, I was alone in the classroom surrounded by the memories of the people's lives I had just touched. It was at this very moment I knew what my calling was. Not only to be a mere cooking instructor, but also to be a messenger of how food can change the quality of the very lives we are all living today.

In this classroom I witnessed, for the very first time, people asking for help. Wanting to educate themselves with the knowledge to make a difference, not only in their kitchens, but also in their lives as well. Sometimes one can get comfortable with the ideas and information in their head, and naively believe that everyone else already knows what you have learned over the years. Getting in front of a group of people brought me to the realization that I have a lot to share.

Since that day, I have taught hundreds of cooking classes, performed countless cooking shows and have spoken to thousands of people about the importance of food and cooking in our existence. It is now time to attempt to bring the most pertinent of that information together in a solitary book... and that result is what you are holding in your hands today.

I wanted to create a book that could be easily taken with you: slipped into a briefcase, a purse, carry-on luggage, etc. In other words, I didn't want to pack it full of "fluff". Between the covers of this book are some profound ideas that I want you to embrace. Feel free to use a high-lighter for certain areas that you want to revisit; fold corners of the pages; underline personally relevant points. There is a lot of useful advice here for you.

Is parsley really world peace in disguise? That is quite a statement. Not just parsley, but food in general is. Food is one denominator that not only do we all have in common, but also it effects our senses and well being on so many levels. No matter what race, religion, or financial status anyone is, we all begin, end, and continue through our days with nourishment. It connects us all together... if we let it, and at the same time enriches our lives and existence.

Why parsley? Parsley is one of the oldest known garnishes. On restaurant plates and in butchers' display cases; although its use may be limited nowadays, the role of the bright green sprigs is ubiquitous. The intention of garnishing a dish or a food item is to add visual appeal. With embellishment, the look of the food is enhanced and is done so to make it more attractive and more tempting. This allurement then leads to anticipation of eating, making one salivate, and the theory is that this will then improve the whole eating experience as we nourish our bodies... making us feel better on so many levels.

The title of this book was chosen to help reflect the amount of influence food and its preparation can have on our day-to-day lives. I didn't want it to be thought of as a cookbook... because it is not. There is not a single recipe to be found in this book. It is however, a guide, a manual if you will, on how we can get food to change, not only the way we look at our plate, but also on how food can assist us in living our lives to the fullest.

This book is for the culinarily skilled, for the ones that struggle with a can opener, and everyone else in between. It is for anyone that loves being in the kitchen and for the ones that detest it, but most importantly it is for everyone who wants to enrich their lives and relationships with an everyday means: food.

We all need fuel for our bodies and chances are you have already eaten something today. Did it enrich a relationship? Did it inspire you? Was it a celebration of flavour complexity? Or was it just a repetitive motion of lifting your hand to your mouth as a monotonous task of keeping your body fueled?

All of our homes are equipped with a kitchen. This, along with some direction, is all you need to change food into a catalyst to bring you a wealth of happiness to enhance your life and relationships.

The Shower Theory

There are many ways that, as we age, we become numb to certain aspects of our existence. When we are born into this world, every interaction is new. Everything we experience is a fresh adventure full of discovery and stimuli. Think of a baby experiencing a new sensation, a new sound or a new flavour. As these experiences become repeated, and even mundane, as we grow and develop, they capture our attention much less. In order to awaken that excitement in all of us now, we have to retrain ourselves to become fully aware of everything that we do.

Take showering for example. We as adults shower every day. Nothing exciting there. Just a monotonous task of our daily hygiene, right? Wrong. I have four children, and one of the many milestones I fondly recall was when each of them reached the age of graduating from the bath to the shower. This was an important time in all of their lives. At the time it was a representation that they were grown up. They even walked differently as the approached the awaiting shower, strutted even. However, I caught myself giggling every time when each of them cried in laughter as they shielded the spraying water from their bodies saying "It tickles!".

"You're a silly goose", I would tell them, "you'll get use to it".

That's the problem: we've gotten *used to it*. That and a million other things in our lives. When was the last time you focused on the spraying water in the shower, and really felt it? Felt the invigorating influence of every stream impacting your body. It takes tremendous amount of focus after all these years of being *used to it* to accomplish this now, but the important point to note here is that it can be done. We can awaken these feelings if we choose to do so, and the spraying water in the shower is only the beginning.

Eating and tasting is no different. For many of us, we've gotten used to it. Don't get me wrong; there are still many times that we eat an incredible meal and we enjoy every bite of it, but there are just as many occasions, if not more, that we don't take notice. Every time we put a morsel of food into our mouths is an opportunity not only to taste, but also to feel, smell, and even see. Everyday our lives are filled with a myriad of opportunities to embrace flavours, textures, aromas and colours. How many times do we fully seize these opportunities?

Food is life, and life is a celebration. To get the most fulfillment and pleasure out of that celebration, we must become fully aware. This will be a very personal and individual journey for each of us, however there are many suggestions that I can give to start you on the right path.

First is the admiration of colours and visual stimuli of the dish. What does the dish look like? What colours and shapes are present? Can you describe the shapes and the shades of the colours? How do these specific shapes and colours interact with other shapes and colours in the dish? This is also an opportunity to build anticipation of what the textures may be like just by looking. For example, does it look like it will be rich, creamy, crispy, chewy, or crunchy? A slight exploration of the dish with your serving utensil will help you to describe what the textures may be like in your mouth, when you do eventually take a bite. What about the shape and colour of the serving plate itself: how does it compliment or detract from the dish?

Undertaking this process may seem intimidating or even pointless, but it is not difficult and it is an imperative first step. With practice of focus you will eventually become fully aware of these components without even trying. Imagine how amazing these components would be to someone who was blind their entire life, and could all of a sudden see for the first time. Don't take this visual procedure for granted or as an opportunity to be critical, just be conscious and aware.

I am certain you have heard of the term "anticipation is half the fun". I am not only suggesting this first visual step to help you appreciate food and meals more, but also to build excitement of the meal before you eat.

Aromas of the food will also help to build your eagerness to start eating.

Lift the dish to your nose, and smell. Inhale deeply and let the fragrance fully encompass your nasal passages. What does it smell like? Is it a familiar aroma and does it trigger anything in your memory of past occasions? What scents can you pick up on and describe? How does it make you feel? The area of the brain that processes smells and aromas is closely linked to the area of the brain that triggers memories and emotions. For example, for me, the smell of a stuffed turkey cooking brings my mind back to a time when I was a child: A Thanksgiving Day in autumn, when I would come in from playing outside to the warmth of the house and the aroma of Mom's turkey in the oven. Sage and the lingering aromas of the fried sausage and onions from preparing the stuffing, danced throughout the house and embraced me like a welcoming friend. We all have memories similar to this just from familiar scents. Take a moment to think of some of yours that stand out in your mind. These experiences can also arise unexpectedly.

17

A scent can suddenly trigger a memory eliciting strong emotions. When this happens, make a point to fully experience it, rather than simply brushing it aside.

~

The more we indulge our senses the more distinguishable aromas will become, and the easier it will be to decipher them. Some will be more prevalent than others every time you eat. Today for instance, I was eating lamb shawarma wrapped up in a pita, with yogurt, lettuce, and tomato. When putting it to my nose the main scent was the yeasty floury scent of the bread. I was expecting the spices of the lamb to prevail over all others, but it was the bread that carried my imagination to a bakery or the warmth of a home with the aroma fresh bread baking. Making a conscious effort to remember to smell your food will solidify this essential practice as an automatic reaction whenever you are about to indulge in any amount of food or beverage.

Many aromas are also released during the cooking process. Take the time to be fully conscious of these scents and how they make you feel. Celebrate the fragrances encompassing your home as you may be creating long lasting scent-memory associations for yourself and/or a family member that they will hold dear to the heart for years to come.

Now, after looking and smelling, it finally comes the time to taste. How is it? A standard mundane answer such as "it's good" is not acceptable. What are you tasting? Why is it good? Take the time to explore and discover flavours in the dish. What ingredients can you taste and recognize? Eating is a celebration of all of our senses and they all play significant roles in the symphony of eating, but "taste" is the one that the majority of people associate with the most when it comes to the enjoyment of their favorite dish or cuisine.

Upon further examination of the "taste" sense, we are able to break it down into four recognizable basic distinctions: sweet, sour, salty and bitter. This dissection however does not capture the taste of such things as steak, potatoes, prawns, asparagus, tuna, and mushrooms for example. In each of these mentioned instances we can recognize that there is a distinct taste to all of these ingredients, but none of them fall into the four previously stated categories of taste. How would you describe the taste of a steak besides using an uncreative term such as "meaty"? This is where the term "umami" comes in as a fifth basic food taste classification.

Umami is Japanese for delicious, but the definition has much more depth than that. Umami is the recognition of a pleasant savory taste that has been impacted by naturally occurring amino acids in food usually signaling the presence of protein. No combination of sweet, sour, salty or bitter can replicate or mimic the taste of umami, and thus it is a basic taste description all in its own. I like to translate that it represents the heartiness in the taste of something. The science of taste suggests that we have these five basic taste senses for a reason. Sweet indicates to our body a source of energy and carbohydrates, salty a source of minerals, sour as evidence that something is not ripe, bitter as a signal that a toxin may be present, and umami signifying protein, an important part of human health.

This act of tasting is also an opportunity to discover textures in the dish. Is it crisp, soft, velvety, rich, crunchy, chewy, fluffy, or flaky?

How would you describe the flavours and textures to someone that was not eating the same meal, without using words that were components of the dish? Do the textures in the meal come close to what you expected them to be from when you examined it earlier with your visual perception?

For example, our family sat down to smell and taste a simple bowl of vanilla yogurt with granola. Everyone had to follow the rules of how to describe it without using the words "yogurt" or "granola". Some of the words that came up in conversation were: crunchy, crisp, tangy, sweet, vanilla, nutty, creamy, smooth, etc. This a lot better than saying "it tastes like yogurt and granola". Getting in the habit of doing this with everything you eat may seem like a bit of a task at first, but this is an integral part of awakening your senses that have probably been asleep for quite some time.

It is also important to recognize contrast: contrast in textures and contrast in flavours. Contrast is when two opposites come together to make what you are eating more exciting, like crunchy & creamy or sweet & sour. The amounts used are balanced with each other, but the results are amazing. The yogurt with the granola example in the paragraph above is a perfect example of crunchy & creamy, and I am sure we have all tasted sweet & sour. There are countless contrasts that can be created and enjoyed and I want you to get in the habit of recognizing them.

This food adornment is not much different from how a trained sommelier inspects and tastes wine, or how a whiskey connoisseur examines and sips single malts. It's about fully appreciating what is being offered to you in every aspect of its existence. I often joke when teaching cooking classes and say "I am here to give you the secret to life: Do It More!" If you want to become good at something in life, do it more. It's really that simple. It doesn't matter if it is bowling, cooking, mowing the lawn, public speaking, playing a musical instrument, or even embracing your senses – the more you do it, the better you get. All jokes aside, this is true, and it is also a lesson I preach to my children. As a part of growing up and learning new things, children get frustrated when they are not good at something, or think something should be easier than it is. What do I tell them? Do it more. If playing piano was easy, everyone would be a pianist. It is those who work hard and persevere that achieve success.

The great thing here, is that I am not asking you to really do anything different in your life than what you are doing already. No need to make time for lessons or meditation. Just be aware of your senses every time you eat or drink something. The more you do it, the better you will become, and the easier it will get... to a point where it is just automatic. Pretty soon it will just become a habit and your life will be more enriched simply by fully experiencing your senses being tantalized many times each day.

Do not overlook the importance of fully seeing, smelling, tasting, and feeling your food. This is the important beginning of your journey to letting a repetitive common denominator in our lives, such as food, be a catalyst to change our lives. Changing ourselves and our opinions by affecting our daily lives in a positive manner is the first step. How can we use food as a positive peace creating means with other people, if we ourselves cannot approach food in this manner first?

You may have noticed that I have left out our fifth sense of hearing for obvious reasons: food normally doesn't make any sounds on its own. However, the sounds of meat sizzling on a hot cast iron dish being brought to the table can definitely heighten our eating anticipation levels. The other obvious situation would be if you were the one preparing the meal and were aware of all the sounds involved in the cooking process. Also hearing people biting into or chewing on something may help you predict the textures that are present. Aside from the fact that hearing people consume their meal is an etiquette foe pas, sound can enhance your meal.

This ability of embracing food with our senses can be done with anything we eat; whether you have prepared it yourself, or someone has prepared it for you; whether it is just a coffee and a scone, or a full seven course gourmet meal; whether you are at a restaurant, or, heaven forbid, opening up a packaged microwaved dinner. You will be surprised at what you can discover and the sensations that have been going unnoticed and unappreciated for so many years.

Invite others to share in this exploration of senses. This will not only introduce them into embracing and enriching their eating/drinking experiences, but will also help you with your progression of mastering this as well. Families that sit down and eat together are a perfect opportunity for this. Perhaps you might try to make it part of speech at the beginning of a special gathering: "Thank you all for coming here today on this special occasion. Before we start eating I want everyone to look at the food on your plate. What do you see? Lift it to your nose and inhale. Etc...." Some may find it trivial or even silly, but if given a chance they will experience an overall improvement in the quality of their lives from something that they do everyday anyway.

If you work as a server at a restaurant, you can do this with your customers as well. Instead of asking "How is everything?", ask more specific or open ended questions like "Can you taste the quality of our free range beef and locally sourced organic vegetables?", or "Wow, your food smells amazing at this table and reminds me of _____. What does it remind you of?" Don't overdo it. You want to help people embrace their meal experience, but you don't want to be a nuisance either.

The natural progression in these approaches of awakening your senses to food and ingredients will also start to enhance your perception in these areas. Furthermore, this will also eventually help to diminish any negative feelings about cooking. Some people thrive on meal preparation and cooking, some detest it, but most are anywhere in between.

One of the most peculiar couples I have ever met approached me after one of my live cooking performances at a local fair. "I can see by watching you that you love to cook." She said. "I can see that the crowd was inspired by your show by their cheers and undivided attention, but my husband and I, we never cook. You could even go as far as saying that we hate to cook, so we never do it. You may think I'm exaggerating, but I'm not. We literally never cook. We eat in restaurants, get take-out, fast food, and buy microwave prepared dinners."

I was shocked, to say the least. My first thought was to ask her "why are you telling me this?" However, before I could, she went on and asked me "I bet you can't guess what we use our oven for?" I shrugged my shoulders and she said "to store cookbooks. It's wasted space for us, so we use it as a bookshelf."

This was the oddest thing I had ever heard. "Why do you even own cookbooks, if you don't cook?" I asked.

"Doesn't everybody?" She replied.

Although I was, and still am, dumbfounded by her answer, she has a really good point. She's right: everyone has a collection of cookbooks, either large or small, including apparently even people that don't cook. I am assuming that they must have received them as gifts?

We all get into cooking ruts at times in our lives and our meals in the meantime suffer from the lack of creativity – you're not alone. You could say that you have gotten *used to it*. However, right there in your own home, you have an assortment of cookbooks just waiting to be opened, explored and utilized. How many cookbooks do you have? How many are used constantly, occasionally, and never at all?

I have a challenge for you. At some point over the next seven days I challenge you to open up one of those cookbooks. Not one that you received as a gift, but one that you purchased yourself with your hard earned money. I want you to relive the moment when you bought it. The moment when you were flipping through the pages with excitement and motivation, saying to yourself "I need to have this book" as you laid your cold hard cash down on the counter. Something in those books, at the time, was inspiring you to get into your kitchen and cook. Find those recipes again, and this time… make them.

Motivation can easily be stimulated from outside sources (such as cookbook recipes in this case), but true motivation comes from within. You have to take that first step, the steps that follow, and the final step to make something happen. If you are truly discouraged with the same old meals you are making, or with your lack of time in the kitchen, you will find a way to make this happen.

Many cookbooks simply just gather dust because we either forget about them, or more likely find that there is too much effort to learn new recipes and we stick with what we know... it's easier. Getting out of our regular routine, and our comfort zone can create anxiety, so more times than not we tend to avoid it.

I guarantee you this however, if you take the steps, and keep trying (even through times of possible mistakes or failures), you will eventually succeed. Your meals will become new again and with any luck you will find happiness in the novelty of the food and cooking techniques you have utilized. Take this success and let it inspire you to keep learning new recipes. Chances are you have a kitchen and plan to continue to eat the rest of your life, so this will not be a waste of your time.

I could at this time also make the suggestion of searching the internet for recipe ideas. However, I think that with the vested interest in the cookbooks you have already purchased, you will be more driven (and in the end, more fulfilled) to create this victory yourself from these resources already at your fingertips.

It is just as important for you to observe your feelings as you are reading this, or whenever you think about cooking; are they positive thoughts or negative? Do you feel inspired or discouraged? Perception of how we see something is very personal, and sometimes can be deeply ingrained in us, but it can be influenced. We will discuss this more in the next chapter but for now I want you to have the mindset that cooking isn't difficult, it is just that you have chosen to not find the time to learn and appreciate it yet. That's it. It's that simple. No need for labels. By removing any negativity, but still taking ownership of our own individual situation, we in turn create a different perspective all together, and this creates an opening.

Be the child that gets tickled by the shower water. You won't regret it.

Cooking is Not Vacuuming

There are many household chores that daunt our daily lives and it sometimes seems it's a never-ending struggle to always balance these chores with other priorities. Let's face it, we all perform many roles in our daily lives such as: employee, parent, spouse, gardener, maid, chauffeur, chef, etc. Unfortunately, somehow in the mix of all of these home responsibilities, the role of chef in many homes has become twisted into a task that we classify along with other jobs such as vacuuming. Although vacuuming is important to the ongoing cleanliness of our homes (I don't want to insult any clean fanatics), it lacks the ability to nourish our bodies, embrace our senses, transform lives and build relationships. In comes the role of home chef.

I have spoken to many people about the happenings in their kitchens on a daily basis and the role that they play in meal preparation. You would be surprised (or maybe you wouldn't) at how many people said that cooking dinner, for example, is their "chore" in the household.

Let's first look at the definition of the word "chore". The Webster's New World College Dictionary states that a chore is "a small routine task, as of a housekeeper or farmer; a hard or unpleasant task".[i] If cooking has become a "hard or unpleasant task" we're in big trouble. Eating and preparing food should be embraced and celebrated for the huge impact it can have on our lives and the people in our lives.

If we approach anything in life as a negative, or if we search for negatives, can you guess what will always be found? That's right... the negatives. Do this simple test right now: Look at someone or something in the same room or area that you are in right now. Maybe it's a person walking past you, or sitting on the same bus as you. Maybe it's your cat or the curtains on the wall. Make this your subject for this exercise. What do you see? Believe it or not, we do have a choice as to what we see. We could choose to look with very discriminating eyes and see all the negatives: "look at those clothes... oh my goodness, did they even look in the mirror before they left home? There's cat hair everywhere – why do I even have a cat? Those curtains are hideous and do nothing for this room; I should just take them down." You looked for negatives and that's what you have found.

Now take this same subject and look for the positives. They could be: "I bet she has many great stories to share about her life. He really seems to be in great physical shape. I love having my cat greet me at the door every day. Maybe if I replaced the curtain rod and pulled back the sides, those curtains would really add some appeal to this room." Simple, right? Be aware of what you are looking for and your experience will always be more rewarding. Try this exercise now with the subject you have chosen.

~

Food and cooking are literally no different than the subject of the exercise you just completed. We have all, at some point in our lives (or always), found the negatives in cooking to a certain degree. Now it is time to eliminate these negatives and replace them with positives to change your approach and opinion about being in the kitchen. There are many ways that preparing and eating meals can transform your life and relationships, but changing your opinion to a positive one is our first step. Even a number of professional Chefs struggle with this as they have prepared food all day, and this may be the last thing they want to deal with when they come home.

Attitude is everything and you are in 100% control of it. This is something that is fact. I'm not saying it is always easy to change your attitude or how something affects your mood, but it can be done. No one else can control how you feel. Take ownership of that. Try to recognize and be aware of the times you are feeling negative about something and see if you can change how you feel. There are times when I notice something is bothering me and I feel like I have a rock in my stomach. I will then stop what I am doing and think about why specifically I am feeling this way. Once I have identified the source of this undesirable feeling, I do my best to change my attitude and look at the situation from an optimistic perspective. The results are positive, more times than not, and my mood, and my day, are enhanced by the steps I have taken to do this. Anytime we can improve our living experiences daily, it is a good thing.

One of the most wonderfully appealing aspects of food is creating and/or eating something completely delicious. Even if you are not the culinary type that craves to unleash your cooking talents in the kitchen, you are still capable of appreciating a recipe simply by tasting it. Food is life, quite literally, because without it we would not survive. Therefore, if you have to eat anyway, why not consciously make efforts to broaden your culinary aspirations.

Let's take the "chore" factor out of the equation for a moment. When was the last time you have eaten something at a restaurant, or been a guest to someone's dinner party, and absolutely loved a certain dish? Whether we believe that we're capable of being successful in the kitchen or not, we are gifted with taste buds that bring us a tremendous amount of pleasure when we come across something incredibly delicious. This is the goal, or end result, of what the person who is preparing the meal is trying to accomplish. This "end result" is much the same as a beautifully performed or written piece of music, or an incredible painting; we can all appreciate it whether we are skilled in that area or not.

Appreciating something is easy, you may be thinking; whether it be music, food or artwork. Creating, on the other hand, needs practice. Let's look at this from a different perspective: Can you paint? I don't mean the walls of your home, I am talking about artwork; oil paints on canvas for example. Can you create beautiful works of art? For most of us, the answer is no. What if you were locked in a room for one year with an endless supply of paints, brushes, blank canvases, etc. Other than food being brought to you daily, and access to washroom facilities, you would be cut off from the rest of the world and have no other responsibilities, other than to paint. What would your paintings look like on day one? For most of us, including myself, not very good. What about the ones on day 365? It would be easy to assume they would be much better; maybe even incredible.

Another way of looking at this situation is for us to assume that in order for us to stay alive, instead of eating, we need to paint at least three times per day. This would be how we, as humans, nourished our body: by painting. Every home would be built with an art studio; it would be mandatory, and we would paint. As we grew older, and continued to paint, day in and day out, would we get better at it? Of course we would. The secret to accomplishing anything in life is very simple: Do it more. Period. That's it. The more we do something, the better we get at it. Apply this to anything and it is true: painting, bowling, writing, mowing the lawn, etc., and yes, even cooking.

Cooking is an art form, much like music or painting, but with three great differences: 1.) We already have a kitchen "studio" in our homes to use on a daily basis, 2.) It does not take years of practice to start creating the simplest of dishes that offer enough flavour complexity to make your taste buds go wild, and 3.) We all need the end result to stay alive and nourish our bodies.

At live cooking shows I have addressed many crowds with two simple questions: "How many of you have kitchens at home?" and "How many of you eat food everyday; possibly three to four times per day?" Yes, the answers are quite obvious, but that is the point. Every home is equipped with a "studio" to prepare meals that we need to rely on in order to stay alive. Even if it is a simple piece of toast with peanut butter, we are still using this facility in our homes and supplying fuel to our bodies. Is the environment welcoming? Do you enjoy the atmosphere in your kitchen? How can one expect to be successful and motivated in an area if it is not appealing?

Let's start by making some simple changes that do not have to be overly expensive. I encounter many situations with people wanting to improve areas of the culinary arts within their home kitchens and lifestyles, and the first and easiest step is removing clutter. A cluttered work area is not inspiring. Many people realize this already with their job workspace, such as a desk or workshop, but the same applies to our kitchens. You need room to not only feel comfortable but also to provide yourself with adequate work space. It is nice to have objects in your kitchen that are of decorative value but make sure that these things are not taking over your kitchen. Keep them to a limit; enough to define you and your style, but not so much that this is all you see. This is your opportunity to get rid of that old stuffed "kitchen witch" ornament your Mother-in-Law gave you back in 1975, and anything else that has been collecting dust over the years.

I recommend doing a complete purge of your kitchen. Remove everything from the counters, above the cupboards, off the top of the refrigerator, and even anything stuck on the refrigerator door. If you have the time, and feel motivated, you may want to take this opportunity to also clean out all your cupboards as well. Once this has been done it will be much easier to see how much welcoming space you have in your kitchen to work with. Now, with a discriminating attitude, only put back the things that are of utmost importance or value to you. This is also a great opportunity to rediscover a kitchen appliance or tool that you haven't used in quite some time. It could possibly be time to either get rid of it, or be the source of great inspiration for some new meals. It's too easy to not get rid of anything because of great intentions, so this type of decision making journey will be a personal one. Be determined, but be realistic at the same time.

The next step is functionality. Keep one area cleared that will be always be used for a cutting board. Or better yet, purchase a beautiful wood cutting board that you will want to leave out all the time. This is one less item to retrieve when it comes to meal preparation time. This newly created cutting area in your kitchen should have easy accessibility to your knives and perhaps your sink and/or stovetop. Knives are best kept in a knife block where they can be easily removed and returned every time you use them. If your counter space does not allow the room for a knife block in the preparation area you have chosen, then consider purchasing a magnetic knife strip that mounts on the wall. Another solution would be a knife holder that slides into a nearby drawer. The main thing to keep in mind is that knives should not be stored loose in a drawer. This is not only dangerous when rummaging through the drawer for the correct instrument or utensil, but also detrimental to extending the life of the sharpness of the blades. If knives are banging around in a drawer, the sharp edge will become dull much faster than if they were protected and kept separate. This is one of the same reasons why knives should never be washed in the dishwasher; jets of water will force them to knock around against the other cutlery, let alone the harshness of the detergent. Knives are investments; your tools of the trade, and should be washed carefully by hand in hot soapy water with a soft cloth.

The next area to focus on is the accessibility of other kitchen utensils and equipment. A canister with an assortment of wooden spoons, spatulas, and other tools works great. You don't need to have every utensil you own in there, just the ones that you use the most. Where your pots and pans are stored is just as important. If you have the space, consider buying a hanging pot rack. This will not only make them more easily accessible but also provide protection to non-stick surfaces by not having them stacked on top of each other in a cupboard. Most pot racks also provide ample storage of lids on the surface above the hanging equipment. The other obvious added bonus of a pot rack is the sudden creation of extra cupboard space. If there is no ideal space for a pot rack in your kitchen, another idea to create space in your cupboards is to install a lid holder on the inside of one of the cupboard doors. It is a simple rack, usually metal, that holds lids vertically on the cupboard door allowing your pots and pans to be nestled together in a stack more easily. There are many more ideas, like revolving caddies, slide out shelves, etc. that you can easily incorporate without spending too much money. Do some research online to get familiar with what is available within your budget.

Some of the best tips in kitchen functionality at home come from the day-to-day operations of a restaurant. In a restaurant scenario, turning a profit at the end of the day is a necessity above everything else. Losing money will not keep you in business no matter the popularity of your venue or food. Labour costs are one of the biggest factors restaurants deal with on a constant basis, so finding streamlined ways in completing the preparation and cooking processes always have a positive effect on profitability. For us at home, thankfully our labour is free, so we will use this comparison as a way to make the processes in our kitchens faster and easier to allow room for more enjoyment. For example, the popularity of having small salt and pepper dishes by your home stovetop was derived from the operations of commercial kitchens. By having these frequently used seasonings literally available at your fingertips, rather than taking them out of a cupboard, you have one less step to take in starting or completing the cooking process. Another tip that is similar to this is to have two squeeze bottles of oils also accompany the space near your stovetop. They can be purchased online or through a local restaurant supply store for very little money. These bottles should be filled with two distinctly different oils: one for salads and low heat cooking methods like an extra virgin olive oil, and the other with a high heat pan-searing oil such as grape-seed oil or rice bran oil. Again, this would bring you one step closer to cooking that much sooner.

Other areas to consider for ease of use would be the accessibility of your spices and pantry. In freeing up the extra cupboard space by purging or installing that pot rack, you now have an opportunity to reorganize the contents and locations of where things can be best stored. You may even want to revamp the state of your pantry and the food supply in your kitchen. Perhaps you have always wanted to have a pantry that is more focused on one or more of your favourite cuisines. For example, someone who loves Mediterranean cuisine would stock their pantry with varying types of olives, capers, tomatoes, grape leaves, olive oils, balsamic vinegars, etc. The refrigerator and freezer can also be coordinated to contain the perishables of the same cuisine. Motivation to focus more on cooking certain cuisines in your household will start with having the ingredients at your fingertips. One can even take this to the extreme in organization by creating labels and segregating areas in your pantry for different food groupings.

Again, this is not about making it a chore. This is about giving you ideas to find ways to inspire you. Everyone is different and not all ideas will seem inspirational to all people. This starts the process of transformation. What ways can you think of that will make your kitchen workspace more functional and welcoming?

~

Organizing or redecorating a space in your home will always entice you to spend more time in that area. You may want to complete your kitchen transformation by hanging some kitchen art or framed posters to create a new theme to your kitchen. This can also be taken to the extreme if your budget allows, by refinishing the cupboards, buying new appliances, and adding a new coat of paint. This amount of work however, is not mandatory for you to feel like your kitchen has become more of a special place. Sometimes all it takes it a little extra lighting to create a more open and inviting space. Easy to install under-cupboard, lights can be found at very reasonable prices. Do some investigative work in this area the next time you are at your local hardware store. Ask the employees for some suggested solutions that are within your budget. They will be able to navigate you through the store, much better than you alone, and introduce you to products that are new and popular.

One of the last, but most important, things to do is ask yourself "what do I love?" A few years ago I met a woman after performing a live cooking show and she approached me with a problem she was struggling with: She didn't enjoy cooking anymore. "I used to like to cook", she said "but now I hate it and I find myself trying to avoid it as much as I can."

So, I asked her that simple question "what do you love?"

She looked at me oddly and said "I'm not sure what you mean?"

I replied "ok, you hate cooking, I got that, but there must be something in your life that you love. What is it? Anything. Something that you love more than anything else."

She thought about it for a moment, then responded by saying "well... I love my horses".

"Great" I said, "what kind of music do you like? ...and what do you like to drink?"

"I love classical and opera music" and she continued with, "...and I like to drink red wine... but I'm not sure where you're going with this?"

"Fantastic" I said, "here's what I want you to do: literally take everything out of your kitchen and only put back things that are of functional value: pots, pans, knives, utensils, dishes, etc. Get rid of all the clutter. I want you to find ways to get your horses into your kitchen, but not literally. Gather together and choose the best photos you have of your horses. Get them framed, enlarged and matted even, if you choose, but find a way to get images of your horses into your kitchen. If you have it in your budget, tear down a portion of a wall to install a window where you can see your horses from your kitchen. The next thing I want you to do is install speakers in your kitchen from which you can play your favourite music - not from the radio as there are too many commercial interruptions; your own personal music collection is best. And finally, every time you have to cook I want you to pour yourself a glass of red wine."

By interjecting a number of things one loves into a process that they hate, chances are they will learn to love the process... or at the very least make it more tolerable. Here is an example that you can try today to prove this theory: The next time there are dishes to clean up in your kitchen, play your favourite music in the kitchen while you are cleaning. Again, not the radio, but your best music choices in the genre that you love the most. You will catch yourself moving to the music, singing or humming, and having a better time than if there was no music. Not only will you be cleaning what is necessary in the process, but also you will be going above and beyond what needs to be cleaned, without even realizing in most cases: the corners, the backsplash, etc. You'll find that you're having an enjoyable time during the process.

Procrastination happens in all aspects of our lives, because we would rather do something that we find pleasing, than something mentally, emotionally or physically distressing. Cooking is no different. If we can find ways to help cooking be more fun and enjoyable then we will have no problem doing it, and some will even look forward to it. However, if we don't like it, along with anything else we don't like to do, then we will put it off as much as possible.

Many people, in order to avoid cooking, will simply talk themselves out of it. By doing so, they make it seem in their minds that it will be a lot more work than it actually is. They will conjure up images and scenarios in their minds until they are at the point where they cannot be bothered. For example, they may say to themselves "I don't have time for all that work; even if I knew what to make, I will still have to do all that chopping and measuring; not to mention all the clean up at the end; I think I'll just order a pizza instead." Once you get up and start cooking, and do it often, you will realize it is really not that much trouble after all.

Even if you think you hate cooking, there are ways to make the experience and surroundings more pleasurable by bringing in the passions that you have in your life. Let's face it, we all need food to stay alive, and unless you are planning on winning it big in the lotto, you will have to cook the majority of that food yourself for the rest of your life. There's no getting around it, so you may as well find a way to make it worth your while psychologically too.

Now that we have your kitchen in a more workable, inviting state, it's time to get you inspired to do some cooking. The simplest of all culinary resolutions would be to blow dust off your cookbooks and start making some new dishes. As mentioned in the previous chapter, whether it is of small or large proportions, we all have collections of cookbooks... with many of them going unused. There was something about each and every cookbook that you bought, that enticed you to purchase it; something that caught your eye, and tantalized your taste buds. What was it? Ask yourself this very important question about each book when you go to revisit this collection of yours.

Make it a long-term goal in your home to open up one of these cookbooks once or twice a week, and try a new recipe. If you choose to do this, make sure you are setting yourself up for success. If you feel that you are culinarily challenged, start with simpler recipes. Decide on and investigate the recipes prior to the date you plan on making them. Read the recipe instructions through a couple of times. Purchase the ingredients ahead of time, and ensure that you have the basic equipment, necessary utensils and the time available to successfully complete the task at hand. This will help eliminate any stress that you may encounter during preparation of the dish.

When working from recipes in your cookbooks, feel free to write on them. Get a pencil (so you can erase too if desired) and make notes regarding ingredients, techniques and/or your opinions on the final results of each dish. This will help your memory in the future when you revisit these recipes and hopefully provide you with more consistent successes with future meals. These are your books, you bought them; it is okay to write in them. Recipes that you have made many times should have "chicken scratch" all over them. You may even have a recipe card collection that you haven't used for quite sometime. Do you remember those: recipe cards? A very archaic system in today's age of technological advances, but many people still have them. What's in that old recipe box? Why are you hanging onto them if you don't use them? There must be some good recipes in there if you have collected and saved them for this long. Maybe this recipe card collection is of sentimental value from a deceased loved one? What better way to honour these people, than to use the recipes that they created and/or collected over their years of existence. Take pride in your decision to do so as these people would have been thrilled to know that they were the source of your motivation and creativity.

Perhaps it is time to make digital versions of these recipe cards. This way you will not only have a more secure way of saving them, but also allow you to more easily make changes to the recipes. Sharing them with friends and family will also be easier. There are many apps available to help keep these newly formatted recipes categorized as well. Having a spot for your tablet or laptop in the kitchen may then become a regular practice.

A great way to add to your cookbook collection, and in turn get some motivation and ideas, is to shop at a second-hand store. I love flipping through the pages of used cookbooks and seeing which recipes were used the most. Some pages will have hand written notes on them, and others will be splattered with food. Some of these cookbooks have recipes that were used so much that the book naturally opens to a certain page because the binding has been worn down. When perusing through these cookbooks I can't help but think of the history

I am holding in my hands: the countless number of family events, special gatherings, and the day-to-day lives of the people that owned them. I always check the publication date and the older and more well used the book, the more my imagination carries me away to the times and places the book could have encountered. While you are at the second-hand store, also check for food magazines. These are very inexpensive and also another great resource for generating some creativity in your kitchen.

If you truly cannot get any inspiration from a cookbook collection, the internet is also a great place to find recipes and instructions for practically any cooking style, cuisine or technique. There are literally thousands of cooking videos at your fingertips for you to learn from. In this day and age there really is no excuse for not knowing how to cook. Maybe choose a food genre (like Italian or Chinese, for example) that you are interested in and start injecting recipes from that genre into your weekly routine until you have mastered some new favorites.

Perhaps there is a dish at a local restaurant that you love? Have you ever thought about trying to recreate it? Again, with all the information available to us at our fingertips, it can possibly be done much more easily than you could ever imagine. Maybe the restaurant Chef will even share some of his/her secrets? There's no harm in asking and chances are they will take your inquiry as a compliment. Obviously because of the very specific outcome you are striving for, this very well could take many recipe attempts on your part to get it exactly perfect, but think of the gratification you will feel when you do. It's important to recognize successes such as these in the kitchen and take the time to recollect and congratulate yourself. Any positive affirmations for your efforts in any aspect of your life, is always a good thing.

I remember when my wife and I found a great restaurant that served the most incredible Indian butter chicken. We loved that dish so much that we started frequenting that establishment on a somewhat regular basis… until we challenged ourselves to recreate it. It took a number of tries, but eventually we not only mastered it, we liked our version even better. That resulting recipe by the way can be found in a couple of my cookbooks.

I also often find inspiration from what's on sale at my local food shops. On many occasions I will challenge myself to create meals with a particular ingredient just because it is on sale. In a way this is easier because I don't have to completely decide on my own what to make. The sale item will steer me down a path that I may not have thought of myself and all I have to do is decide what to do with that ingredient. This is another example of where the internet can be so helpful.

Another inspirational start would be to search for cooking classes available in your area. If you decide to attend a cooking class, make sure that you ask questions. It is your hard earned money that you are spending and you want to be as confident as possible when starting something new. Find a Chef that you can connect with or relate to and learn as much as possible. If a business is offering cooking classes, chances are that they have a number of Chefs focusing on many different cuisines for you to choose from. Do your homework and make the best choice for you.

If I had a dollar for every time I heard someone say that cooking is a chore, I would be a rich man. The act of cooking a meal is just that: "cooking a meal". It is not negative, or even positive for that matter, it is just something we do.

We all need food to stay alive and since our homes are all equipped with kitchens, we cook. Maybe some of us more than others but we all still cook. Some kitchens will have their owner's unharnessed culinary passions bestowed upon them on a daily basis, while the only glory days in other kitchens may be derived from someone adding onions and garlic to a saucepan of store bought pasta sauce… but it is all still cooking.

I hate to even imagine that there is a percentage of our population that rely on daily practices of consuming products like TV dinners, frozen pizzas, and spray can pancake batter. Yes, I did say "spray can pancake batter"! Talking with employees of a large grocery chain, they tell me that they are constantly bombarded with requests from consumers for fast already prepared meals that they just heat & serve. Is there really such a growing number of people in our society that have succumbed to rely on pre-made meals from a package or container. Have we lost so much time in our ever growing busy lifestyles that we cannot commit to practicing creativity in the one life-nourishing art form that our homes have always been designed around?

Who made cooking negative anyway? We did. We did as human beings. Take for example the simple tasks of washing a vehicle, mowing the lawn, or our daily commute to work. Are these tasks of complete negativity that all of us are destined to suffer through for the rest of our lives? No, some of us thrive in these situations. What makes these tasks at hand, along with cooking, a chore then? Our perception is the answer: how we perceive these things. It really is that simple.

One of the things that we do, that no other life form does, is analyze and label. Practically every single thing we do, other than breathe or blink, we analyze and label. We create good and bad, positive and negative with our natural human psyche without even realizing it for the most part. Cooking, again, is just cooking. If it is positive for one and also negative at the same time for another, it is because each of those persons have made it so. It is individual opinion or perception that makes the act of doing something a joyous occasion or a nagging daily occurrence.

Don't get me wrong; people are entitled to their opinions, and if there are people out there that are happy with cooking being a chore, then so be it. What I don't want is people believing that they don't have a choice of it being a chore. Of course you have a choice. You just need to find the way to create a positive frame of mind regarding the task at hand. So with cooking, in our home, we introduce music and a favorite beverage to the environment and use this as an enjoyable opportunity to catch up with each other and take pleasure in the family being together in one room.

Everyone is unique however, and what seems to be a simple change of focus to creative optimistic endeavors with one person, may need to be completely different for someone else. What makes you happy? What can you bring into the kitchen environment (mentally or physically) in order to make a more optimistic approach to this life essential assignment?

~

Whatever it takes for you to have a more positive approach, the truth is that you will typically save money and eat healthier overall for doing so... and hopefully enjoy yourself, your family and your kitchen more.

Our society is bombarded with artificial solutions to our hectic lives, such as fast food restaurants and pre-made, prepackaged meals. It is a sad state of reality when quick and nutritious meals are only an idea away. Yes, some planning needs to be involved, but it is not as difficult as one may first think.

Slow cookers are the most obvious answer and many recipes can be found at your local library or on the internet. I was astounded when I first saw a commercial recently that advertised a prepackaged slow-cooker meal: one that is easily emptied from the bag frozen into your crock pot. Yes, this is still better than deep fried fast-food, but it is basic cooking masquerading as a pre-packaged meal. Not only is it costing you much more in comparison to making it yourself, you also have no control of any preservatives that may be included.

Casseroles are another resolution and very popular with kids. Again this requires some planning, but the most time efficient method would be to prepare two or three casseroles of the same dish at once. This would allow you to freeze the extra meals for an even quicker solution to your busiest evenings. Other dishes that could fall under this same category would be meatloaves, lasagna, shepherd's pies, cabbage rolls, etc. For dishes to be made in abundance and kept frozen, find the day of the week that works best for you, like a Sunday afternoon for example.

Our family will do this on many occasions: on a Sunday we will barbecue up enough meat to last for about 4 days. Then throughout our busy work week our dinner prep is minimal; throw a quick salad together to accompany the protein, toss some of the meat into an impromptu pasta dish or stir-fry, or on our busiest of evenings just throw together a quick sandwich.

There are many other non-casserole recipes that can be prepared ahead of time as well like pasta sauces, pizzas, stir-frys, etc. See what you can come up with that will work for your lifestyle, but have fun doing it. Remember, your opinion of the task at hand is just a perception.

Food is not only an avenue to keep us alive, but it is an opportunity to celebrate life, nutrition, and the joys of flavours. Learning many cooking techniques are great to assist you in the kitchen by increasing your skill set, but nothing can replace the hands-on experience of practice. Cook, be happy, know that you will make mistakes along the way, and enjoy life. Life is too short to get stressed out by a serving of food that is not perfect.

Bringing People Together

With a quick glance at your calendar you will notice that there are many events, such as birthdays, statutory holidays, and casual appointments that are intertwined in our yearly routines. Food, more often than not, is the foundation of those events.

Can you imagine a birthday without a cake? Or a Christmas or Thanksgiving holiday without an evening dinner? Even casual meetings with family or friends usually focus around a coffee or lunch.

Food is, has been, and always will be, the stimulus that is present in these surroundings where relationships are formed, nurtured, and cherished. Let's face it: eating is a very social activity and it has a way of bringing people together. Let's examine this connection in other scenarios that aren't as obvious as the events mentioned above.

Bringing food to a new neighbour is a tradition that has been passed down through many generations, and although it seems to be more of a dying trend these days, there are still a few survivors who make good practice of this die-hard tradition. These gifts are seen as not only a symbol of welcoming, but also a peace offering; a breaking of the bread. When was the last time (if ever) you have partaken in such an offering? What's stopping you from doing so? What harm will it bring?

Maybe you are afraid that it seems a bit personal to offer someone, a stranger really, something that was homemade? Perhaps you could first break the ice with a purchased item from a local bakery, until you know the neighbor better. Let's face it, we would all be somewhat uncomfortable eating a homemade treat from a complete stranger. The only difference is knowing where both you and they live brings in accountability. Now that we have lived in the same house for many years, my wife and I bring food to our neighbours quite regularly. There is nothing to lose and everything to gain in creating happiness with the people that live in close proximity.

One event that is growing in popularity, is randomly paying for the purchase of the next person in line at a coffee shop or fast food restaurant. We, as a society, have coined this as an act of "paying it forward" (when in actual fact we are paying it backward). A way to give or create happiness without expecting anything in return. More often than not however, this act of kindness is done at a drive-thru because the purchase amount for that person in question is already known, and it's completely selfless: you are gone by the time that person gets the surprise. This instance therefore does nothing to build, or create, a relationship or connection, but still uses food or drink to bring joy to someone's life and improve that moment in their day. For all we know, that one single act of kindness could be the best part of that stranger's day, and be the catalyst for them to bring joy, consciously or not, to other lives.

With the life sustaining power of food, you can also touch the lives of people who are less fortunate. Many times I have assisted homeless people by buying them a hot lunch or giving them a bag of food from the local grocery store, rather than giving them money. This way I know without a doubt that I made a difference in their life by helping to nourish their body. This humanitarian act creates a dual value both for them and myself: I have given with the certainty that I am not supporting a vice and they have received nourishment. Other opportunities in your community may include being able to donate to, or volunteer in, a food kitchen or food bank. This could be through a local church or community center. It's in our nature to help others and finding ways to accomplish this will generate feelings of kindness, gratitude, and love… both for the people you are helping and for yourself.

A gift of food for a friend or relative that has fallen ill or been injured is another great example of how to nurture a relationship. Alternatively, that gift of nourishment may be intended to help someone cope during a time of grieving or to mend a relationship. This edible gesture of kindness is often viewed as a greater gift than one of monetary value. The value lies in the thought process and the time taken to carry out such a task, while providing sustenance at the same time. I remember a friend once had a terrible flu and I surprised her with a pot of homemade chicken soup. To avoid her feeling obligated to invite me in to share the meal, I simply left it on her doorstep and called once I was driving away.

Food can also be utilized as a way of expressing thanks. I remember being a child and going carolling at Christmastime with a collection box for charity. My friend and I would go from door to door, bundled up from the cold weather, using each home's outer entryway as our temporary stage. Talk about a dying tradition. I miss those times of unharnessed love for the spirit of the season in a time when we felt completely safe and secure to share that unannounced affection with complete strangers. The greatest memories I have of these outings were the occasions when we were given morsels of food as a way of saying thanks for the moment of seasonal enlightenment that we brought to their household. It wasn't about the quantity; usually just small enough to consume before we got to the next house. Nor was it about that they made it especially for us; obviously we couldn't have been there long enough for them to do so. It was solely about the sharing of what they had and the feeling of peace and love that that act of kindness represented. Don't get me wrong, as a kid I would have also been thrilled if I was given a dollar or two for my pocket as well as the charity box, but it would not have had the same heartfelt meaning. Those dollars would have been spent and forgotten along with the memory of even getting them in the first place. Yet, still to this day, I remember the food.

Even my youngest son can relate to this from the days of working his newspaper route.

There were times when he was given tips of cash as a way of saying thanks for his courteous service, but the gifts of food are what he remembers the most. Both circumstances of getting cash or food as a gratuity was very rare, and the latter even more so. As a matter of fact, there was just one house out of all the houses he delivered to that had ever offered him food. The occupants of that residence were a sweet older couple and it started with a jar of homemade jam. The bargain that was offered to him was that if he brought the empty jar back, he would receive another new, filled jar. This went on for quite some time until they moved away, but yet still to this day we remember that exact house and those kind people, whereas the specifics of the people that gave him money, and the proximity of the homes they lived in, have been forgotten. The cash gifts were never underappreciated, but they were never poignant enough to create any long lasting ripple effect in his life.

Let's look at this from a different angle. My wife is a teacher at our local elementary school and for staff meetings and such, she will often bring a platter of baked goods to share with her fellow colleagues. Would it have the same effect if she gave everyone in the room a dollar instead? Or what about if there was more effort contributed than that and she went to a discount store and bought everybody a trinket, like a paperweight or a pen? Not only would these be looked upon as odd gestures of camaraderie, they just wouldn't have the same affect. The emotional bearing of the platter of homemade goodies being offered has a much more far reaching impact on our human psyche. Not only are the staff members being offered a substance of nourishment at the end of a long workday, but it is also enjoyment that they can experience and embrace immediately; this brings a level of entertainment to an otherwise possibly tedious meeting as they awaken and enlighten their senses from the act of eating. The mental and physical satisfaction that lingers afterwards is much more meaningful than a trinket that will just be set aside, or stuffed in a pocket or a purse, for later.

The same holds true for the gathering of people at your home. Whether it's a formal champagne event, or just a friendly get-together with friends and loved ones. Even the simplest of appetizers are very social and a must for any successful party. The myriad of flavours offered by the different dishes, and leisurely mingling and grazing upon them by your guests, helps to fuel conversations and the feeling of contentment. There are so many outlets for one to buy appetizers pre-made from the freezer section, but this eliminates all the creativity and reduces the level of meaningfulness. Preparing for an evening of guests should be enjoyable and what you prepare should be an expression of your personality. There are numerous options that are not only delicious, but easy as well.

For fancier events, it is nice to have small morsels of food that people can manage with one hand to "pop" into their mouths. This is extremely helpful when a drink is being held in the other hand and there is an abundance of standing and socializing. A perfect example of this would be canapés. Don't let the fancy French name scare you. They are simply pronounced (can ah pays) and are defined as bite-size open-faced sandwiches. Most canapés consist of a base, a spread, and a garnish. Get the bakery to slice your bread lengthwise and toast these sheets of bread in the oven. Then symmetrically place small dollops of spread on every square inch and cut the bread into the squares that are now mapped out. Garnish each one and place them on a platter. An example of a spread and garnish would be horseradish flavoured cream cheese with small pieces of thin beef and a parsley sprig.

For more casual events, chicken wings are an extremely popular appetizer. The price difference of ones that are already "flavoured and cooked" compared to raw ones is drastic. A simple marinade or sauce can be made from ingredients you most likely have in your refrigerator already like barbeque sauce, ketchup, or hot sauce, mixed with a variety of other ingredients. Half the fun is creating something uniquely yours. Nothing is more satisfying than hearing someone say, "Wow, have you tried Bob's wings? They're incredible!" The other half of the fun is all the money you will save.

A suggestion for a very extraordinary appetizer would be an Italian antipasto platter. This can be easily assembled as a last minute dish with a collection of morsels normally found in an Italian pantry. Make a quick marinade of equal parts of balsamic vinegar and extra virgin olive oil for artichoke hearts, tomatoes, grilled asparagus, roasted peppers, or any other vegetables you prefer. Arrange these marinated veggies on a platter along with sundried tomatoes, melon pieces wrapped in prosciutto, roasted garlic heads, chunks of Parmesan cheese, and slices of baguette, for example.

The possibilities are endless, so be creative. Food has a great social aspect of bringing people together, and even more wonderful when you have made it from scratch. This will make your guests feel not only welcome in your home but also more comfortable that they are appreciated by your efforts. Would this be classified as comfort food then?

We have all heard of the term "comfort food". We in fact have all craved it, smelled the aromas in anticipation, and of course eaten it. What is "comfort food" though, exactly? Is it only big bowls of stew-ish type foods on a cold winter day that one eats while wearing pants with a stretchy waistband? Does it exist in climates where it is warm year-round? Comfort food can be, and is, whatever you want it to be by what it means to you. That's the beauty of it; if by eating it, it gives you a level of comfort, be it physical or emotional, then it can be considered comfort food.

The physical contentment from eating comfort foods would be the warmth felt by the temperature of the dish, or the spiciness of it, and/or even the mouthfeel of the richness about it. However, pairing these physical sensations with the psychological satisfaction from eating something considered to be a comfort food, is where I think the true definition lies within people and where the pleasure really comes from.

Comfort food can be a dish that stirs up sentimental feelings for example. Maybe a certain aroma and corresponding flavour is linked to a memory of a place once visited, a special time or celebration in one's life, or of a beloved person. Recipes of a nostalgic nature may also be classified as comfort foods. Foods from a certain time period or specific culture that trigger emotions may be enough to sanction it into this classification. For instance, on the 17th of March when our table is filled with classic Irish dishes, it not only feels more fitting, but also fulfilling... or comforting. This is just one example of many celebrations that could include, but not limited to: Asian delights on Chinese New Year, incredible Indian food on Diwali, or haggis on Robbie Burns Day... yes, there are people that consider even haggis to be comfort food. For those of you not in the Scottish culinary loop, haggis can be defined as a savoury pudding containing a sheep's organs (heart, liver, and lungs for example) and combined with onion, oatmeal, and spices traditionally encased in the sheep's stomach and simmered. I am actually quite fond of it myself on occasion as long as it is served warm; once it gets cold I find the texture loses its appeal.

The feel good sensation of comfort food can also be obtained by simply loving the taste of something, maybe by that of your favourite type of food or favourite recipe. This literally could translate into almost anything for any one individual. Basically foods that make you feel good because you are consuming something you love to eat. The act of doing so would bring on positive emotions and help to suppress negative feelings, and that alone could be enough to be considered comfort food. So, comfort food can be, and is, anything you want it to be, as long as it makes you happy for one reason or another... even if it is just temporary.

Food as a meal is also used to enhance, or set the mood for, a romantic relationship. Take Valentine's Day for example. Trying to make dinner reservations on an evening when ninety percent of the general population is also trying to attain the same goal is not my idea of fun. You may be able to perform this feat without pulling out your hair, but if bustling crowds and hurried serving staff is not your idea of romance, one can easily create this setting in the comfort of your home.

Staying in for a romantic dinner can be accomplished with little effort and some creative planning. To achieve this successfully, let's look at three areas to focus on: the menu, the table setting, and the room environment.

The menu you decide on does not have to be complicated, however it should be meaningful. Your effort should reflect the love you have for this person. The first thought that comes to mind is to prepare their favorite food. If this is a dish that is not within your ability to prepare at home, then have it ordered in or pre-purchase parts of it ahead of time to ease your preparation. It's acceptable to not have everything prepared from scratch if it is beyond your means and capability. Your thoughtfulness is the most meaningful ingredient.

Add extra simple courses, rather than just having a main course and dessert. Once again this does not have to be perplexing. A fresh pile of mixed colourful greens with a good dressing makes a great salad course. A few pieces of unique cheeses with some grapes and a small glass of wine make another delicious course. All of the elements to make these extra courses can be purchased direct from the store and assembled to ease your preparation. Now you can express to your sweetheart that you made them a "four course romantic dinner". An example of a quick enchanting dessert would be chocolate covered strawberries.

A situation like this may also be the perfect occasion to serve some aphrodisiacs. These are foods that psychologically and/or scientifically help us feel... well "in the mood" for lack of more appropriate words. The search of the perfect combination is the desire for many on dates such as Valentine's Day. Although each person's own food preferences play the biggest influence on this romantic journey of cuisine, there are some classic ingredients that fall into this category.

The first ingredient that comes to mind is chocolate, and I am certain that many will agree. With its velvety smooth melting texture, and the perfect balance of sweet, salty, and bitter, this addition to dessert choices will usually win over any other. Chocolate has also been scientifically proven to contain ingredients such as phenylethylamine and serotonin: two chemicals that stimulate pleasure senses in the brain. This, plus the natural stimulant effect from the caffeine, makes for a wonderfully seductive and addictive ingredient.

Oysters and caviar have also been considered aphrodisiacs for many years, and some argue it is because they are a good source of zinc, which contributes to maintaining male potency and fertility. However, there are many other foods high in zinc that are not considered aphrodisiacs such as lima beans, lentils and spinach; and I don't believe making your Sweetheart a stir-fry of these ingredients will give any kind of romantic impression.

Cayenne pepper and spicy foods also play large roles as aphrodisiacs because they increase heart rates, blood flow, and perspiration. Some say that endorphins are also released during this process and thus give one a natural high and pleasurable feeling.

Champagne or sparkling wine is considered the drink of lovers, but one can also use nonalcoholic sparkling grape juice as an alternative. Alcohol can lower one's inhibitions and thus be regarded as an aphrodisiac, but the tiny bubbles, even in nonalcoholic alternatives, are said to be very seductive.

Regardless of what you choose to serve, there is one last ingredient I should mention that is also believed to be an aphrodisiac: garlic... when eaten by both people. It may be, however, considered a prophylactic when eaten by just one.

The romantic table setting is very important and should harmonize with the mood you are trying to establish. Candles are a must, but there are other things you can do to make it memorable. Silk rose petals or heart-shaped confetti scattered on the table is a nice touch. Compliment that with red cloth napkins and a love letter tied up with a ribbon, and you will have them swooning. Make sure you have enough pieces of cutlery set to accommodate each course and use your best wine glasses. A glass of wine always looks very elegant; if wine is not desirable, then fill the glass with red juice. A finishing touch on the table would be a fresh bouquet of flowers. Long stemmed red roses are a perfect symbol of love, however they will be impressed already by your efforts and carnations or a mixed arrangement should do just fine.

The room environment is equally influential. If you have children, make arrangements for them to spend the evening, or at least part of it, with Grandparents or doing other appropriate activities. Be certain that you serve dinner in a light controlled room and have access to music. Your music collection is the best option as they eliminate the hassle of having to listen to advertisements on the radio. Lastly, make sure that the room is tidy. It is much harder to set a mood if the area is cluttered with everyday items.

These are all great ways to transform your dinner experience into a special event, but what about breakfast? Isn't this the most important meal of the day? Yes, to most health professionals it is, so I feel compelled to dedicate some ideas to making that pinnacle feast into something remarkable. I do understand however, that a vast percentage of the population have "day jobs" and that making a spectacular breakfast on a weekday is far from being at the top of your priority list. These ideas are more geared towards your days off or if you work evenings.

This is the perfect circumstance to forget about the bowl of cold cereal or toast and jam, and try something new. One of my wife's favorite breakfast pastimes is making and perfecting different pancake recipes from around the world. It seems that every walk of life has their own version of what we know as the traditional North American pancake. Making it a ritual to do a different pancake recipe every Saturday or Sunday morning is a fantastic journey around the culinary world.

French toast is another common "special" breakfast that many people enjoy, but we prepare it differently on many instances. Instead of the traditional method of dipping bread in batter and frying in a pan, we often will make a large casserole dish of French toast the night before, letting the egg mixture soak in, and then baking it the next morning. Not only is it an extraordinary display at the breakfast table, it also allows us to have more free time in the morning to sip our special coffees and enjoy each other's company. Actually there are many recipes that you can get mostly prepared the night before, like muffins or biscuits for example. Measure and combine all of the dry ingredients and then all you have to do is incorporate the wet ingredients in the morning.

Incorporating fresh baked breads or unique types of bread will also enhance an ordinary breakfast. One way to make this easy is to prep the loaf the evening before, cover with plastic wrap and store in the refrigerator overnight. The bread might rise slightly in the fridge, but you will need to remove it from the fridge an hour or two before baking. Remove the plastic wrap, let it rise in a warm place until it doubles its original size and bake as usual. On many occasions we will serve fresh baked bread simply topped with butter and honey.

If all of this seems like "work" however, there is one very quick way to help transform your regular breakfast of cold cereal: top with a handful of fresh in-season berries or some slices of banana. This will take very little time, offer more flavor, nutrition, and make a better presentation. There is a reason why all the photos of cereal on the cereal boxes are like this: better presentation has more mouth-watering appeal, and thus equals more of a chance of you buying it.

Picnics can be another area of focus. Do memories of bland potato salads and boring sandwiches persuade you to buy fast food or, worse yet, keep you locked indoors? Whether it's a romantic picnic for two or a family outing, easy to prepare gourmet ideas will liven up your picnic basket for any nature excursions you have planned.

One of the simplest things to pack for a romantic picnic for two is a fruit and cheese assortment, as there is virtually no preparation required. A grocery store with a delicatessen counter will be able to provide you with a number of small cheeses and specialty meats. While you are there pick up an assortment of fruit like grapes, pears, and local fresh berries, along with some gourmet crackers and pepper jelly. Wash the fruit but leave everything else in its original store packaging. You will want to pack a small cutting board, a couple of sharp knives and, if legally feasible, a bottle of wine. If wine is not an option, then juice in wine glasses will create the same seductive ambiance.

Too many family picnic gatherings are bombarded with the consistently usual potato salads and coleslaws. However, no matter what salad you choose, it will require some assembly, so one is better off expending that energy by making something different. The variations of salads are endless. A quick and easy way is to create one from the ingredients you already have in your fridge and pantry. If you don't have the creativity confidence to go this far, then a quick search on the internet should result in a popular recipe you have never made before. Whatever salad you choose to prepare, pita pockets are the perfect item to serve them in. They will eliminate the need for paper plates and plastic cutlery, while adding a gourmet aura to your salad eating experience. If carbohydrates are a concern, lettuce leaves also work great as salad holders.

That brings our conversation to the next common picnic item – sandwiches. Instead of peanut butter & jelly or egg salad, why not make Italian pressed sandwiches filled with a variety of Mediterranean meats, cheeses, and complimentary flavours. This is not as hard as it sounds, as it is made in a large loaf and then cut into individual sandwiches. To ease the preparation, purchase a large Ciabatta loaf from the bakery counter. Cut it in half length-wise, and hollow out the majority of the center while keeping the shape of the outside crust intact. You should be able to put the top back on and have it look like an untouched loaf. Fill the center with layers of a variety of sliced meats like salami and capicolli with a complimenting cheese like provolone or shavings of Parmigiano Reggiano. Continue to fill the bread with gourmet olives, sundried tomatoes, capers, fresh basil and oregano, salt, fresh cracked pepper, and some extra-virgin olive oil. Put the top of the bread back on, seal it tightly with plastic wrap and refrigerate overnight with a cutting board and some heavy cans placed on top of it to press it all together combining the flavours.

These are just examples of how you can tailor any meal to be more special, but don't stop with just these examples. Find ways to make every day, common weekday meals at home more extraordinary as well. Make it a habit to use a tablecloth or cloth napkins for every meal or take a second thought about using your fine china or crystal more often. Most of us seem to have these dining keepsakes that we treasure but seldom use. Life is for living and these treasures should be used and celebrated with the ones you love. If you don't have such a collection, or face constraints in your budget, second-hand stores and garage sales are great resources, especially if you enjoy hunting for these treasures. Make it fun, but elaborate, and your reward will be the enhanced experiences at the dinner table.

You may even want to turn the actual meal preparation time into a way to enhance relationships. This can be done with anyone at any time. Preparing and cooking a meal in your household collectively is an opportunity to catch up with loved ones while you share responsibilities of bringing that meal together. Put on some music, pour a favourite drink and enjoy each other's company. Finding opportunities for families and couples to cook together is just as important as making it a priority to eat together. If there are children involved, this also becomes just as much as an opportunity for learning as it does for nurturing your relationship with them.

Using this idea of cooking together with friends and loved ones can also help to relieve the stress of cooking during busy work weeks. A "cooking party" with close friends or family is when you all get together to make a bunch of food and at the end divide it amongst yourselves to be stored and used in the future. Perhaps an event like this is arranged because one of the people involved has a cooking or baking skill they would enjoy sharing with others. Regardless, it is another opportunity to nurture the relationships you have in your life already or maybe even to create some new ones.

The most important suggestion overall is to be aware and conscious of food/people interactions and find ways to enhance or create them.

Silly Parent, Food is for Kids

Recently my Mom turned 80 years old. We held a large birthday celebration for her and I was called upon to address the crowd with my recollections of her life. This is kind of ironic actually, because I am the one that has caused her the most pain on that date in history: I was born on her birthday.

I took great pride telling the stories of my childhood that made an impact on my life and who I have become today. As a child, my Mom was the biggest influence on my life. Being a single parent of four children for numerous years, she persevered through many of life's obstacles to ensure a suitable developmental environment for all of us. There are many examples of her dedication to motherhood, but the fire of culinary aspirations that she fueled within me is something for which I am forever grateful.

From my earliest memories, she was always there to offer me a spot beside her in the kitchen. While other boys my age were involved in various sports activities, my idea of a team was her and I in the kitchen of our home. Still to this day, I can almost hear the scuffing of the old wooden footstool as I dragged it across the floor. There I would stand proudly upon the flour-dusted crevices as she secured my apron readying me for our next culinary adventure.

Many of our kitchen conversations were a journey back in time. Descriptive adventures of what life was like when she was a child, were what I loved the most. Her parents migrated to Canada from Germany in the early 1930's and they worked the land as farmers in Saskatchewan. Stories of the brutally cold winters and how most of their meals came from their crops and the pigs that they raised always kept me captivated.

As a child, she too was always by her mom's side in the kitchen. It was there that she gained the culinary skills and confidence that were passed on to me. Many of the meals that I enjoyed as a child were influenced by, not only her German heritage, but also by the underprivileged lifestyle of fortuneless farmers. Creative simplicity was always the focus as we transformed everyday ingredients into something incredible. Some of the most memorable foods for me that stimulate thoughts of my childhood are rice pudding, cherry soup, and sugared milk bread slices.

Now as a father of four children myself, I look back and realize how much work and dedication she had in raising the same size family on her own. It is these memories that have provoked such respect for her. She has not only given me the influence that has created my whole career, but she has also given me the strength, courage and empathy that I need to be the best parent I can be.

This is not to say she or I have never made any mistakes in parenting; we all have at some point. This is to say that she has taught me how to love. I have learned from her that in the long run the most important thing we can do for our children is to make sure they realize that we are there for them, no matter what. There is no problem too enormous for parental love to deal with. No one is perfect, but acknowledging our own mistakes with grace and respect teaches our children to be gracious themselves.

Teaching kitchen skills to our children will not only prepare them for a future on their own, it will also generate openings to create memories and grow the bond between parent and child. Food and food preparation are necessities of life and again this is a wonderful opportunity to transform a parental obligation into a nurturing situation.

If disarray or lack of control in your kitchen bothers you, you need to find ways to let go of those idiosyncrasies. These are barriers that exist only in thought form; they are not tangible. They are not only keeping you from enjoying the development of your child's life skills, but also keeping them from the cultivation of great future memories.

All of this however, must start with a positive outlook on cooking from you first. Kids are clever and they are highly influenced by the actions of those they love the most: you. Whether you want them to or not, they will learn everything from you and your actions: the good, the bad, and the ugly. An optimistic outlook on contributing to family meal preparation is what we are in search of here. Give a child a chance to help in the kitchen and it will not only be the start of a life altering skill, it will also create a sense of pride of what's being served at the table and thus an anticipation of mealtime. Remember the Shower Theory we discussed in chapter one? We, as adults, may have become bored with, and immune to, the simpler culinary pleasures of life. Perhaps experiencing the routines with the fresh point of view of a child can reawaken our gastronomic experience. It will be our children's experience of cooking that will reinvigorate the tedium for us.

Watch them explore. See how mesmerized they become with kneading bread dough or stirring colours together. Ask them to describe what they are feeling, seeing, and smelling. Teach them simple but essential tips that we take for granted, such as: how to crack an egg, or to hold the bowl with one hand while mixing/stirring with the other, so it doesn't tip over. Remember this is all just second-nature to most of us. In passing on your own knowledge (in spite of how un-extraordinary you may feel it to be) you will realize just how much skill and knowledge you actually possess.

The best way to instill culinary passions in children is to make it fun and educational at the same time. For the most part, these will be new experiences for your child, so their interest will be piqued to be begin with, but it will be the fun that will carry them through. Cooking is art, math and science all in one; a complete classroom to enjoy. There are endless resources online for food science experiments that can be done with your child – take advantage of them. Measuring and multiplying recipes will become math lessons and the textures, colours and plating will be the art.

Contrary to popular childish belief, macaroni & cheese, and pancakes, don't come from a box. Teach children to make these from scratch! It is our society, and in many cases us as parents, that have taught them to expect these foods, and countless others, to originate from packages. Kids weren't born knowing that these types of convenience foods even exist and this is an opportunity in disguise. Make it a game to find a food product that comes in a box or a can and challenge yourselves to recreate it together. Taste the differences together and talk about what flavours, textures, smells and colours you are experiencing and discuss why.

Doing exercises like this is also an opportunity to talk about what is healthy, what is not, and why. Remember, this is a life skill that could affect how they eat for a very long time. This will not only get them used to eating healthy food from an early age, but hopefully it will get them excited about a healthy lifestyle too. By the time they reach school age, it would be great if they were proud about opening up nutritious lunches in the classroom instead of wanting, or expecting, junk food all the time.

Packing kids lunches however is a chore for many, and sometimes one can lose sight of nutritional value due to heavily marketed convenience foods. School-time snacks and lunches are not exactly the best avenue to practice "gourmet cuisine", but I do get asked on occasion for some healthy ideas.

Nuts in moderation are a very nutritious option, as long as allergy restrictions aren't a concern. Nuts are a good source of protein and a great source of unsaturated fat (the good kind of fat). Unsaturated fats have been proven to help reduce levels of LDL-cholesterol (the bad cholesterol) without lowering HDL-cholesterol (the good one). Unsaturated fats are best described as the ones that are liquid at room temperature, while saturated fats are solid. Additionally, there are a large variety of nuts to choose from for discriminating tastes: almonds, cashews, peanuts, etc. Some are even available with different flavourings to make them more appealing, but keep your eye on the ingredients and sodium levels of these. Also try to stay away from the chocolate coated nuts the most you can; that will defeat the healthful purpose and make the non-chocolate coated ones less appealing.

Fresh fruit is an obvious choice, but make sure it is something that they enjoy, to increase the probability of consumption. One thing you can do to make fruit more tempting is do some of the prep ahead of time. For example, a cut and/or peeled orange is much easier for them to eat than a whole orange. Make it interesting − don't always send the same fruit. Every once in a while, pack some berries, seasonal fruit, or something exotic like longan fruit (what my kids refer to as dragon eyes). Just make sure they know how to eat anything new; being aware of seeds, pits or inedible skins, etc. Try to stay away from processed fruits, however. Apple sauce and fruit cocktail cups, while better than no fruit at all, are not ideal. Fruit leather or dehydrated fruit bars also have to be chosen with care. Opt for the more natural, less processed, versions and keep in mind that these sticky treats are not good for teeth. Pack them only as an occasional treat. The ease of eating dried fruit makes it an attractive option as well. There are so many naturally dried fruit options that do not contain additional sugar, that it is easy to make their lunch interesting for them. There are dried plums, apples, apricots, pineapple, mango, and banana to name a few, and they are healthier substitutions for pre-packaged fruit rolls.

Carbohydrate type snack options could be granola bars or popcorn. When purchasing granola bars, read the ingredients to monitor the amount of preservatives and refined sugar they include. Do not choose chocolate covered bars as they also, like chocolate coated nuts, defeat the purpose of making a healthy choice to begin with. In general, the harder granola bars are usually healthier than the softer ones. Popcorn, as long as it not drenched in butter, is a great option and a good source of fiber. It is obviously okay (and recommended) that our children consume fat in their diets as it is all part of brain development. Fat intakes should be monitored but not eliminated.

Whole-wheat crackers are another healthy option. Again this may require reading a few labels, but a perfect opportunity to replace amounts of white flour in their diets with whole wheat. For those of you who have time, there are even cracker recipes that you can prepare together with your children at home. The appeal of whole-wheat crackers will be much greater with the pride that comes along with making them. Throw in some cheese slices as part of their dairy products, along with some lean meat slices or tuna salad for their own homemade "snack-packs".

For the record, my title is Chef; not Dietician, Nutritionist, or even Doctor, and these suggestions are merely that. I feel that it is our job as parents to keep educated. Contacting a dietitian, for proper moderations for your children's balanced diets of all the food groups, is highly recommended, or at least refer to trusted online resources for guidelines. I am merely making suggestions to give parents alternatives to the store bought, preservative laden, substitutes they may be buying in the first place. As a Chef, while some of my food may contain a few ingredients that are not the epitome of heath food, my food is made fresh and from scratch.

I am the father of four beautiful and healthy children and eating a balanced diet is of utmost importance with our day to day meals. We also treat food as a celebration however, and make sure that we interject with dishes that are considered splurges, that are in no means meant to be eaten on a regular basis. This is another teachable moment and I feel is a big part of what parenting is about. When I am writing on a focus of this nature, I am also assuming that parents can make these types of specific decisions for themselves.

If ingredients in a recipe you use are a concern, try swapping them out for healthy alternatives. Recipes are not written in stone; they are opportunities for you to practice creativity and learn how to change recipes to suit specific tastes and healthy diet aspirations.

It is not only the cooking and creating processes that kids are intrigued with, but the planning processes and eating experiences too. All of these can create incredible memories for them that will last a lifetime. Find opportunities not only in the kitchen and at the table, but wherever food is involved where you can embrace life together.

Maybe this is the year that you plant a garden, or give your existing garden a makeover. Get your children or grandchildren involved in this. Talk to them about what they would like to grow and maybe even dedicate a section of the garden for them solely. Bring them to the store to help pick out the seeds and soil. Do online research together and make it a team effort. Talk to the merchants at the farmer's market about growing tips and suggestions for the climate in your area. Anytime you can spend quality time with children, create more enthusiasm about eating vegetables, or bring any meal together as a family, offers a lifetime of ripple effects.

Grocery shopping also offers other educational lessons such as planning, nutrition, budgeting and creativity. Get them to help you plan the home meals, make shopping lists together all while following a food budget and a balanced diet of ingredients. Teach them about prioritizing the weekly meals based on your household schedule and ask them for advice; make them feel involved and important in these decisions.

As parents we try to find ways to embrace food in many different environments. Going on a family hike with a picnic lunch is one our favorites. Nourishing our bodies while surrounded by nature can create incredible moments and talking about the food and the environment will help ingrain these occasions into memories that will last a lifetime. The great thing about kids is that the food doesn't have to be complicated. Don't think of this as a chore. The picnic lunch can be as simple or complicated as you want it to be and the adventure for your children will still be as wonderful as ever.

For example, I created a memory for my son Noah in the most simple and primitive of all meals, that I know he will hold onto for the rest of his life. He was about five years old and we had a father-and-son project of a 1965 Ford Mustang in the garage. There was an opportunity for him and I to spend a whole day in the garage together working on it; my wife had to work and his younger sister was in daycare for the day, so it was just him and me. I asked him "if you could have anything for lunch while we worked on the car, anything at all, what would it be?" His answer? "Drink root beer and eat chunks of ham with knives like pirates do!" So that's what we did. I'm not sure that I felt like a pirate as we pierced chunks of cured meat with butter knives, but he sure did. Of course my wife made sure we had an assortment of raw veggies to supplement our meal, but it was a very simple meal, made into a long-lasting memory.

What can you do with your children to create memories like this? Talk to them and let them have some input. You may be surprised at not only what they say, but also how simple of a task it may be for you.

Be Proud of Your Tastes

One of the aspects of the food & wine industry, that I have realized over the years of my career as a Chef, is that people can be so serious. Yes, I take pride in what I do and I think that the role I play in the industry has an impact on people's lives, but why am I expected to have a heavy weighted approach in discussions regarding food and drink?

Many of you probably agree that there are numerous people in the food industry, that we may label as *Foodies*, who come across as pretentious or even pompous. This is perhaps why it is presumably expected for others to be the same way. Don't get me wrong – I believe it is a wonderful thing when someone loves what they do, even to the point where their lives are utterly consumed with related passion, but why must we take such a ridged approach?

Yes, there are rules in cooking, and many are steadfast, but I am talking more about the areas where approaches are not as strict and could very easily be bent based on personal preferences and taste.

For example, I am sure that you have heard the statement that "medium-rare" is the optimal doneness for cooking a beef steak... but what happens when someone likes their steak more done? Or when a person does not like their pasta cooked *al dente* (Italian for "to the tooth" meaning not to overcook; it should have some firmness)? Is it our role as Chefs to tell that person that they are wrong? Or when someone enjoys a Riesling wine paired with their meal when a Sommelier believes that is completely incorrect and only an oily Viognier is the way to go. Or should condemnation be delivered to one that enjoys ice in their single malt scotch? Where is the line where the steadfast rules and training stop and where personal taste and preferences start?

Where that line is and the boldness of that line, varies in many circumstances; but it does exist, and I believe as an industry expert that it cannot be ignored, or overruled, just for the sole reason that we are professionally trained. I remember working with a Chef in my training days that told me: "An individual of the general public has personal preference and taste buds that cannot be ignored. We must not only learn from them, but also learn to accept their perspectives as a part of our ongoing training and fine-tuning of our careers as Chefs. Everyone has an opinion and is a unique individual and should be respected as such." Wise words well said that I have shaped my career around.

I am a fully certified Red Seal Chef, but to me my trades paper is just that: paper. I see myself more as a Chef for the home cook. A Chef for the majority of the households filled with all classes of people, with or without families, that are looking for great meals that are not constructed from obscure ingredients. Meals that are not paired with unfamiliar varieties of wine. If you love food and love to cook, regardless of whether you are professionally trained or not, you are a Chef in my eyes. Does that mean I don't respect, appreciate or value my certification as a Chef, or other professionals in the industry? Of course not. It means that I can find importance with what we have and at the same time be open enough to appreciate and respect others and their opinions. Opinions are like taste buds – everybody has them.

Sometimes the lack of self confidence keeping us from experimenting in the kitchen is not from our lack of skill, but from our obscure tastes. Some people who are considered to be very picky eaters find it much harder to get inspired to cook as they may feel that their opinions on food and food choices may not be correct. This should be the last thing keeping you from the kitchen. We need to recognize that everyone is different and our tastes are what makes us so individual and unique. As a Chef, I have been trained to accept people's opinions, not as criticisms, but as reflections of their personal tastes. It is important for me to then keep an unofficial tally of the results for my own sense of direction.

Let me share a story with you that happened years ago in a hotel restaurant. I was working the beef carving station at the large Saturday night buffet, and as each patron approached me with their plate I would always ask of their desired doneness. On this particular evening, a small elderly lady approached me with a slight look of anxiety.

"Good evening," I said welcomingly, "What doneness would you like?"

Looking around from side to side, wringing her hands together, she bent over and quietly said "I know it's not the right way, but I would like an extra well-done piece."

I smiled and then asked her "What do you enjoy?"

She looked very puzzled and repeated, "extra well-done."

"Then how is that the wrong way?" I questioned.

Sometimes people get wrapped up in the "textbook" ways of the world and if their preferences don't match these rules, they feel quite undermined or disappointed with themselves. It is small conflicts like this that keep some people from expanding their culinary home menu and learning more about food and cooking. We need to realize that everyone is unique in all ways, including their taste buds, and accept the fact there cannot be written rules for all situations. If I were to give this elderly lady a "textbook" medium-rare piece of beef, would she be happy? Would she enjoy it? The answered is obvious.

Here is another experiment for you. Go to the highest-end steakhouse in your area and order the filet mignon or chateaubriand (two cuts from the beef tenderloin) and ask for it to be cooked extra-well done. Chances are they will not prepare it for you and ask you to make a different selection or request. If this happens, what I want you to do is leave. We need to remind these Chefs and restaurant owners that the only reason they are even in business is because of you: the paying customer. If vacating tables is what we need to do to accomplish this, then so be it.

This situation should be handled in a completely different manner. If such a selection and request from the menu is made, then the customer should be given an explanation of why this is not preferred by the Chef and/or kitchen staff. Since the restaurant is deciding to act upon their kitchen/food knowledge to refuse the request, they should use this situation as an opportunity to share their expertise. Ideally the Chef, or a member of the kitchen staff, should approach the table and explain.

For example, "I understand that you have requested the filet mignon extra well done. The filet mignon and chateaubriand cuts both come from the beef tenderloin and although very tender, it is also extremely lean. Fat is not only flavour, but moisture too, and cooking these particular cuts to an extra well done state will result in a very dry finished product. If this degree of doneness is what you prefer, then I would suggest going with a cut that is well marbled with fat such as a rib-eye or even a strip loin. However, if the extra-well done filet mignon is what you want, we will prepare that for you."

This approach is very different and honours the customer. The food opinion of the Chef/kitchen staff has been comprised of years of kitchen training, and an explanation of why they believe their outlook is correct, needs to be communicated to the customer. In other words, they approach the table and share their food knowledge with the consumer. After doing so, it would be appropriate at this time to offer a different selection based on this knowledge that they just shared, but ultimately in the end honouring their menu selection no matter what it is.

As we cook more often and expose ourselves more to the wonderful world of cuisine and cooking, we will not only become more educated on different techniques, but also the "whys" as well.

Have you ever come across a recipe with an ingredient you didn't recognize? What did you do then? Did you go on a wild goose chase for the mysterious ingredient or just pass on the recipe altogether and move onto a different one? I guess it would depend on how obscure the ingredient was. However, with the internet virtually at our fingertips the answer is only a few clicks away.

One of my pet peeves is when I come across a recipe that doesn't lend itself to the average home Chef. I understand that the culinary landscape has changed over the years and will continue to do so. I also understand the desire for Chefs writing these recipes to fill the niche in the market of people wanting to expand their culinary horizons. However, even more so, I believe that these recipes should be meant to inspire the average home Chef by providing descriptions or alternative ingredient suggestions. As a recipe writer myself, I want to make sure that my recipes are approachable by people of all levels of culinary skills.

Before I continue, let me give you an example. I came across a recipe in a magazine recently for a side dish with one of the ingredients listed as "haricots vert". Now because of my experience as a Chef, and since I know a bit of French, I realize that these are green beans. When I first saw "haricots vert" listed as an ingredient years ago I thought "How pompous! Why don't they just list these as Green Beans? Is it because it sounds fancier, more gourmet perhaps, by listing them as Haricots Vert?" But the answer is not that simple: Haricots Vert are French Green Beans. They are longer and thinner than their North American counterpart that we are all familiar with.

I, myself, have never seen haricots vert at my local grocery store or even at specialty produce markets where I live. I have seen however, green beans that were very thin and long, but still labeled as green beans on the bin. Were these actually green beans or haricots vert in disguise due to inept personnel in the produce section? I don't think the problem lies with the markets, but with the recipe creators. The one writing the recipe should include an explanation of any ingredient that may not be recognizable by the average person. In this specific case, maybe they should have suggested a substitution of North American green beans.

Over the years I have seen this many times with many ingredients, but I chose to focus on haricot vert not only because I saw it recently, but also because it is something that can be very easily substituted for. Green beans are definitely not as obscure as other ingredients I have seen such as: sweetbreads (animal glands), foie gras (duck or goose liver), or veal cheeks (self-explanatory, but not of the gluteus maximus variety).

Another view is the marketing aspect of these recipes. For example, a recipe may sound more gourmet if the title of the recipe is called "a Bisque" instead of a soup, "a Demi-glaze" instead of a gravy, or even "Haricot Vert Almondine" instead of green beans with almonds. This doesn't excuse however that the actual ingredient list, or the instructions of the recipe, is not easy to interpret. What would be the harm in making it easier for a broader scope of the population to understand? If anything, it would make the recipe more approachable and more people would make it, and if the recipe was any good they would then share it with others. Passing the culinary success of a Chef's recipe on to others is never a bad thing... in fact one could say it was good marketing.

Let's get back to basics and just make recipes and food that taste good. By this I don't mean that we should all be subject to making meatloaf, chicken breasts, and macaroni & cheese the rest of our lives. I think we should all expand our culinary horizons and boundaries within our means, as (to borrow an old cliché) variety is the spice of life. I think we, as Chefs and recipe creators, should have it in our visions to include people from all walks of culinary skills in the process of our recipe writing to make it easier for everyone to delve further into the culinary arts.

I do feel compelled however to mention that this is just my opinion; nothing more or nothing less. Now excuse me as I am off to make some "Macaroni au Fromage" for my children.

Have Cream, Just Not Every Day

When contemplating the topics and chapters for this book, I knew I had to include my views on the health aspect of food and lifestyle. How can one create peace in the world if one cannot create peace within themselves? Food can not only make you, but it can also break you. I have been there. Having a background, myself, of being overweight at times as a child and young adult, I know that it was not the preferred way for me to journey through life.

I cringe when I think back about the abuse I put my body through because of my terrible eating habits. When I was a young adult, it was nothing to polish off an entire large pizza by myself. I didn't think twice about it: it tasted good so I indulged. All-you-can eat buffets were also on my list of regular routines and I would always challenge myself to seeing how much damage I could do to the food supply being offered... never once contemplating the damage I was doing to myself in the meantime. The people that only know me in the body and frame of mind that I am in today, would never believe these confessions. And although it is difficult to recall these times of gluttony, the memories act as beneficial reminders of how not to go through life, and of how grateful I am for my health and well-being.

I do not dwell on these recollections however; I just keep them tucked away in the back of my mind and bring them out of hiding when necessary. These are not demons, lurking and waiting to obliterate my sound judgement, they are just things that have happened; things I did to myself. That's it and nothing more. I have accepted this and moved on.

Today, between a balanced diet and my best effort at keeping up a regular exercise routine, I have more energy and feel better than I ever did in my younger years. The main difference, more than any time prior in my life, is that I now focus on moderation and restraint more than anything else. There is flavour to be found in all types of ingredients, recipes, and cuisines, and to find greatness in your regular diet is to rejoice in variety and self-control.

This being said, there are countless recipes and food combinations to experiment with. Most menus that I have taught at my classes and shows tend to have had a balance about them. My opinion on life is a bit biased as a Chef, but I believe that food helps us to celebrate and enjoy our daily existence. We need food to survive, so let's make it exciting and something to look forward to every day, but also in a way that is most beneficial to our health as well. By cooking from scratch you have the ability to control ingredients, cooking techniques and also save money. Honing this skill, in the kitchen that you already have, and with the daily requirement that you need food to stay alive, will prove to be invaluable.

If you have ever attended one of my cooking classes or cooking shows, you know that I am a big advocate for using fat in cooking. You will always hear me chanting "Fat is Flavour; Fat is Moisture; Fat is your Friend". I even take it one step further by joking that "My title is not Doctor, Dietician, or Nutritionist – my title is Chef" …but, I always take a moment from this celebration of overindulgence in fat to mention moderation and healthy choices.

If I was to demonstrate an incredibly tasty recipe loaded with fat grams and calories, it does not mean that I would expect you to eat like this on a regular basis. Rich recipes are meant to be illustrated as a trusted component of a special occasion menu when you want to "wow" people with your cooking. They are meant to be paired with side dishes that are more nutritious in the complete scope of the meal, for a more balanced and healthy eating experience.

You literally have one body to last you a lifetime, so it is extremely important to eat healthy and take the best possible care of that body. Overall, what we put into our bodies represents how much we care about ourselves. Both exercise and nutrition, or a lack thereof, is a reflection of the attention (good or bad) we give to our bodies. Ultimately our mindset and mental health are also greatly affected by the lifestyle choices we make and become transparent in our own personal sense of self-esteem.

Food can make or break your lifestyle, your feeling of self-worth, and your dignity. In previous chapters we have mentioned that food is truly a celebration of living, but control and awareness must prevail in the end. Moderation is truly the key. Have cream, just not every day… or if it is every day, then keep it to a minimum. In other words: restriction and portion size. Indulging in forbidden foods should not be done on a daily basis, but if it is, portions size should be observed. Everyone's definition of "forbidden" is different so I will leave it up to you to decide what falls into this category. Whether you practice restriction and/or portion size will depend on your lifestyle, beliefs, and ultimately what works for you to lead a healthy way of life.

This is not about comparing yourselves to others. That is one of the most detrimental things we can do to our self-worth. The problem is that we are inundated with images of what is perceived as perfect and attractive through all sorts of media and advertising. I remember standing in a line-up at a grocery store cashier and visually perusing the magazine covers as I waited. A popular national magazine headline caught my attention: "The Sexiest Man Alive" published along with a photo of an actor. My first thought was "who decides this stuff?" I then turned to a man standing behind me in the line-up, pointed at this magazine and said "Obviously they have never been to our hometown to meet us." We both got a good chuckle out of it. Being conceded is not what I am suggesting here. Everyone has their own beauty. This is about respect for you, your body and the life you have been blessed with. This is about how <u>you</u> feel, both physically and mentally, not about <u>how you think you should feel</u> based on other lives.

Every life, every upbringing, and every path that each of us travels in life is completely different and unique to anyone else on this planet. Life is too short to be worrying about how we compare to others. Life is meant to embrace others, to love one another, and at the same time to love ourselves. The next time you are in a public area, take a moment to look around. Become aware that all of these other people are on journeys all their own; each has a reality that no one else can even start to imagine what it entails. An expedition through life that has brought them to this very day and has made them precisely who they are in both mind and body. We need to become conscious that it is not only okay to be different and beautiful in our own special ways, but also to cherish that. Envision what a different world this would be if each and every one of us could embrace and practice this philosophy.

Now that we have put comparisons to the side, what I want you to focus on is you. Regardless of what other people are doing and looking like, there is a level of health and healthy lifestyle we should be applying to our bodies and existence. Let go of the mindset to be perfect and eat perfectly. I want you to practice mindful and peaceful eating. Doing this comprises everything we talked about in the first chapter about being aware of our senses, but also includes a more psychological approach. Enjoy what you are doing for your body. You are not only refueling your body, you are being cognizant of the process and appreciative of the benefits. Sit, relax, chew, and breathe; do not rush. Put down your eating utensil between bites. Put less food on your plate than you normally do; you can always go back for more if you feel it is necessary. Embark upon each table sitting as a connection of mind, body and spirit. Try to feel your body absorbing the nutrition you are supplying to it, and find ways to celebrate those feelings with positive affirmations. We are able to be in full control of what we do and think, but far too often we are not aware of this, and what this leads to is unconscious eating and an unconscious lifestyle.

We need to take ownership our actions and lives and put ourselves behind the steering wheel once again. When we are born we have no preconceived notions of what is good or bad, healthy or unhealthy, and harmful or beneficial. We adapt all of this from our surroundings, our experiences, and the ideas and thoughts we are subjected to in our lives. If you are not satisfied with the outcome of these proceedings, then it is time for you to step back in and take control. Your life is not meant to be a white knuckled pilgrimage of chaos; it should be a representation of mastery and triumph... for ourselves and our own benefit; not for anyone else.

Let me ask you a simple question: How do you feel when I mention the word "diet"? Do you have the urge to plug your ears and start repeating "la, la, la, la, I can't hear you"? If you've ever struggled with your weight, you know exactly what I'm referring to. There is a reason the word "diet" starts with the word "die": you feel like you're going to every time you're on one.

This is why I don't "diet". The mental insinuations of dieting are too restrictive. It is human nature to yearn for something more when we can't, or don't allow ourselves to, have it. This is why I believe that "dieting" does not work long-term. My family and I call it "lifestyle" instead, implying a lifestyle of making healthy choices. It is not just the suggestion of switching an poorly-implied word with a happy-go-lucky word that makes it better; it is the awareness and actions that correspond to that change. If we were to eliminate certain foods from what we eat, or follow a "diet" that suggested the same, we would crave these abolished provisions even more; it's natural; it's human nature. Instead, we eat what we want, when we want, but we become very conscious of our choices at all times. Every instance when you lift food to your mouth, you are choosing to do so – it is really that simple.

During the year of 2000, from January to June, I lost 50 pounds. I went from 235 pounds to 185 in those six months. For the most part, all I did was become aware of what I was choosing to put in my mouth. I remember the eve of the big New Year's celebration in 1999 very vividly. The evening's festivities were all planned and I was dressed up in my suit and tie and I felt like a stuffed sausage. Tugging at the collar of my dress shirt with hopes of making it feel more comfortable and lessening the reveal of my double chin, I headed to the bathroom to step on the scale. The needle spun around to 235 pounds. On the days previous, I had always just accepted whatever the scale relayed back to me. As ludicrous as it sounds, I never thought I had a choice. This night however, was different; at that very moment I realized I did have a choice. I realized that I was the only one lifting food to my mouth, and choosing what that food would be, and how much. No one else was making those decisions for me; I was doing this to myself and I was devastated.

My biggest weakness back in those days was a specific brand and flavour of tortilla chips. If I had to eliminate those specific chips from my daily eating regime, I would have yearned for them even more; I was that addicted to them. The way I solved this problem still took willpower but it worked for me. I always had a bag of these on hand, and had just one single chip per day. Yes, you read that correctly: just one chip per day. Every day when it was time for me to indulge in that one chip I would open the bag, take out that one chip, and then reseal the bag and put it away. I would then take my one chip, walk away from the kitchen, and say the following to myself: "This represents my weakness. My goal to be healthy is more important than these chips. I am choosing to have only one because I have the strength and willpower to do so. I am in control of my life and well being. I am choosing to only have one because I can always have another one tomorrow." I had this privately written out on a note to myself in my pocket and it wasn't long before I memorized it.

For me, this is what worked. I was still able to eat what I enjoyed and achieve my healthy eating and exercise goals at the same time. Were there days that I had more than one chip? Yes, but very rarely. If I did happen to have more than one, then I usually stopped myself at the fourth or fifth chip because I was conscious of what I was doing. The other important aspect of this is that I never spoiled myself with that one chip when I was hungry; it was always shortly after having a balanced healthy meal. Again, this is what worked for me and what works for you may be completely different. Was it difficult? Of course it was, but anything that is worth achieving does not tend to come easy. Today I cannot even remember the last time I had one of these specific chips that I was so addicted to. I had eventually eliminated them from my life because of this new found self control.

If this sounds too difficult for you, then instead try to have one splurge meal per week.

This way you won't feel like you are eliminating pleasurable foods forever. If you get a craving for something unhealthy, just say to yourself "I am going to have that for my splurge meal this week". Keep in mind that temptations may happen more often than not, so it is best to keep it to one splurge per week and plan to have that splurge at the end of the week. This is not only to congratulate yourself at the week's end, but also you will have the chance to have it earlier if something unavoidable comes up. The more you set yourself up for success (having healthy food options available to you at all times for example), the better your outcome will be.

One of the troubles of North American society is that food is so abundant that it has become a form of entertainment. We are not only entertained by the act of going out for dinner and socializing for example, but also by the pleasing sensations from the act of eating itself. Everyone is uniquely individual and how this impacts anyone will be different from person to person. It is important to not lose sight of how enjoyable food and eating can be, but instead try creating positive emotions about the aspects of eating that are better suited to the lifestyle you would rather have, or the one you are maintaining. The battle is mostly mental.

~

"Make a choice to eat well as much as possible because chances are you will live longer and have a better quality of life because of these choices."

~

People always subconsciously choose to avoid pain (emotional or physical) and always gravitate towards pleasure. Again, it is human nature to do so. It's quite straightforward actually; I would rather feel good, than feel bad. If you can find a way in your mind to compute your healthy lifestyle as pleasurable, your chances of success are much greater. Obviously this is easier said than done, but taking the time and effort to realize, and identify with, the good you are doing for yourself is an admirable first step. Incremental and modest beginning changes to your eating habits will help you solidify this new frame of mind. Small steps like these are just that, but the increased number of small steps one takes, the greater the distance one will travel. Do not attempt to make leaps and bounds from the start of this new vigilant awareness; drastic measures will fail more often than not.

I would like to introduce you to what I call "The Rocky Theory". I love the movie series of boxing champion, Rocky, and after watching one of these films I have the urge to head straight to the gym and attempt to work out well beyond my capabilities. Motivation to get you moving in the right direction is good, but if overdone it can ruin your long term success. If your body is not used to extreme exercising or even extreme dieting, then you will do more damage than good if you are over-motivated. Don't get me wrong; it is great to have motivation, but it is also important to be aware of your limitations during the process. Too many people enter aspects of healthy eating and exercise with an all-or-nothing type of attitude. We get so determined that we create plans of execution with very high expectations and lofty goals with unrealistic time constraints. Unfortunately, instead of getting all of what we want to achieve, it leads to nothing more times than not. This all-or-nothing mentality sets us up for failure almost every time because we set unrealistic goals and don't allow ourselves any forgiveness when we stray off the strict regimen.

Keep your lifestyle routine attainable by knowing what is realistic in the current stage of your journey and what is not. This way there will be many small successes along the way to celebrate instead facing failure. As time progresses you can reassess your goals and set new attainable levels of achievement that are reasonable and sensible.

Don't be overwhelmed by your long term goal. Stay in the moment of what you are doing right now. Just take this moment into consideration and do what you can in this moment to keep on track. Then do the same in the next moment, the one after that, and so on. Our days are comprised of many opportunities for success, but if we are always focused on how monumental our long term goal is, it will seem overwhelming and unattainable. I do this for exercising as well. When I am on the treadmill for example, and I have a 20-minute workout ahead of me, I break it down into moments that I can wrap my head around. Instead of thinking that I have to get through 20 minutes, I break it down in my mind that I only have ten two-minute segments to do. I then say to myself "surely I can do 2 minutes" and keep repeating that mantra as I countdown from ten to my last two-minute segment.

Take it moment by moment and day by day and focus on what counts: this moment right now. Nothing else matters. Do what you can in these moments today only. Tomorrow will be another "today" full of new moments to embrace. Yesterday was also comprised of moments, but try to only recognize and congratulate yourself on the positive ones and don't worry about the others. Worry has no constructive place in our lives. I try to be aware of my feelings and if I catch myself worrying about anything I ask myself a simple question: "can I do anything about it?" If the answer is "yes", then I do it. If the answer is "no", then I do my best to let it go, and this helps me to not worry. Seems too simple to be true, but with practice and focus it will lead you down a better path.

To help you achieve confident focus, write notes to yourself as gentle reminders to the mindset you should be in. A quick search on the internet of positive, inspirational, or spiritual quotes is a great way to get started. Find ones that really connect for you; ones that have an impact on your emotions. If you feel self-conscious about distributing these expressions throughout your house in plain view, then find a number of hidden away spots that will even surprise you at times: in books, drawers, gloveboxes, storage containers, taped inside cupboard doors, and even tucked into the visor mirror of your car.

I speculate that we all want to be healthy to a certain degree, and obviously some more than others, but the beginning of a new calendar year is always a testament to this opinion of mine. Every January, one will notice an onslaught of extra people at the gym or on local outdoor running tracks. Included in the top 10 most common New Year's resolutions are *lose weight, exercise more,* and *eat better.* Although I am not a Dietician or a Personal Fitness Trainer, I can assist you in the kitchen to a certain degree from a Chef's perspective. Obtaining new cooking methods and ideas that will help to add variety and excitement in your meals is sometimes all it takes to be successful when applied gradually to our daily eating habits. Let's be honest, how many more boiled eggs, dry pieces of toast, or plain salads can you stomach before you lose your resistance to the burger and fries that haunt your dreams?

Here are a few simple helpful tips to get you motivated in the area of daily cuisine:

1. Try different low fat cooking methods such as grilling, poaching, and non-stick sautéing. Having a backyard barbeque is a popular event during the summer, but year-round, it provides a great low fat cooking method. Grilled meats, fish, and even vegetables always taste great because of the distinctive flame-licked smoky taste and caramelization. Very little fat needs to be added to keep these items from sticking and there are no pots & pans to clean up. A low-fat cooking spray applied to the cold grill before igniting can also ease the cooking process and help to make those wonderful grill-marks. Another idea is to dredge proteins in spice rubs before grilling to help prevent sticking.

2. Poaching in a savory no-fat broth is a great way to not only infuse flavour, but also keep your chicken or fish

extremely moist. I find that poaching is very misunderstood; It is not the same as "boiling". One of the last things I would want to eat is boiled chicken. The culinary definition of poaching is to cook gently in water or other liquid that is hot but not actually bubbling, about 160 to 180 degrees Fahrenheit. "Sous Vide" cooking is also growing in popularity and worth mentioning here as well. It is a water bath device that cooks food, vacuum sealed in bags, at specific temperatures. Unlike poaching, the water does not have direct contact with the food, and cooking can be done at any temperature that your device can be set to. Keep in mind that sous vide cooking does not provide the opportunity to infuse flavours from the liquid. In many cases, proteins that are cooked using a sous vide technique are marinated in the bag or seared afterwards for a flavourful crust.

3. Braising meats is another way of reducing the amount of fat in your

meal. "Braising" is the process of quickly browning your meat for flavour and then cooking covered with a small amount of liquid. Inexpensive tougher cuts of meat that are cooked using this "moist heat" method over a longer cooking time will become very tender. The liquid (wine, broth, beer, juice, etc.) helps to break down the unpalatable connective tissue found in these bargain provisions from the butcher's counter. However, braising also works with leaner products like round steaks, skinless chicken breasts or pork loin – just don't cook them as long. Regardless, always pay attention to the ingredients in the braising liquid so you are aware of the nutritional aspect (calories, sugar, sodium, fat, etc.) that you are subjecting your protein to.

4. Quite often it is what we add to our food that is fattening rather than the food itself. A suggestion would be to try topping your main course with a no-fat salsa. This can be made traditionally with tomatoes as the

base, or the contrasting flavour appeal of a fruit salsa on your steak, chicken, or seafood. If this sounds like too much preparation, there are pre-made jarred varieties available (just make sure you read the ingredient list). If salsas don't entice your appetite, then try making different sauces from ingredients like no-fat, high protein Greek yogurt. Many recipes for these types of applications are available on the internet.

5. An easy way to reduce your daily intake of fat is by making small changes to the items you consume regularly. Take milk for example. Let's assume you want to make the switch from homogenized to skim milk, but you feel the change is too drastic. Make the transition by taking small gradual steps to achieve this goal. For the first month make the switch from homogenized (which is over 3% milk fat) to 2% milk until you get used to it. On the second month switch from 2% to 1%, and then 1% to skim. Within three

months you will have succeeded without making a huge adjustment. This is just an illustration for argument sake only, because I know of many with the opinion that some no-fat products, like skim milk for example, are not healthy for you. So rather, maybe your goal is to convert to coconut milk, almond milk, or soy milk instead: make the transition slowly by starting with small amounts incorporated into regular milk and over time increase the concentration.

6. Another suggestion, with caution, is the abundant number of no-fat bottled dressings in your local supermarket. They are not only for salads, but for busy lifestyles use them as marinades, dips, and sauces with certain dishes to help add variety quickly... just always remember "no fat" doesn't mean "no calorie" or even "healthy"– always read the nutrition labels. You might find hidden sugars, starches, sodium, and artificial preservatives which are used to make up for flavour and consistency loss resulting from fat

removal. Please keep in mind that using fresh ingredients and preparing meals from scratch is always the best method for optimal flavour and ingredient control. Suggestions of premade packaged products, if used, should only be in moderation and if your life seems too busy at first to cope otherwise.

7. Most importantly, when preparing a meal, make sure you garnish. This is extremely important for enjoying and experiencing food to the fullest. Eating is not just about taste, texture, and aroma – it is also about appearance. I always preach to my culinary students "the eyes eat first". If something looks great, you are sending signals to your brain advising that it's going to taste great. The same happens in reverse. If someone serves you a bowl of gray colored mush, it doesn't matter how good it might taste, you have already convinced yourself that it will be terrible.

~

I find it amusing that the old saying goes "never trust a skinny Chef", implying that the Chef's food can't be very good if the creator of the food doesn't eat very much of it. A skinny Chef rather, should be looked upon as one who can not only control their passion for food, but also knows how to make healthy food taste great. Not only am I conscious of what (and how much) I am putting into my body; we also have a home gym to help facilitate a balanced healthy lifestyle. I will be the first to say that my job has the occupational hazard of constant food sampling, but I also believe that what goes in needs to be burned off.

In a very basic approach, if our goal is to lose weight we need to increase the number of calories burned daily, while keeping our diet maintained at the current level. This can also be interpreted as we can alternatively decrease our intake of calories, while keeping our exercising (or lack thereof) at the current level, for the same affect. The increase in your exercise level however, is the better choice of the two as it will lead to better cardiovascular health and an increase in lean muscle tissue, among many other great benefits. A combination of both lifestyle changes will obviously have the benefit of producing faster results.

Regardless, a great way to reduce the number of calories you eat is to consume more of what are classified as "negative calorie" or "zero calorie" foods. These can be described as foods that take just as much, or more, energy to chew and digest the food than the number of calories that are in the food. Although there may be no hard fact scientific studies to prove this to be true, these types of foods are definitely low in calories and also very nutritious. Some examples of these would be celery, broccoli, cabbage, spinach, garlic, and cucumbers. Of course what you put on these foods, or how you cook them, can add a lot of calories.

Healthy eating food guides recommend that we, as adults, should be eating an average of seven to ten servings of fruits and vegetables every day. Children should be eating four to eight servings, depending on their age. This is an ongoing challenge for some people, so to assist you I have gathered some beneficial ways to help fulfill your intake requirements for healthy eating. Please keep in mind that I am not a dietician and these are merely suggestions from a Chef's perspective.

A single serving of fruit or vegetables can be described as one half cup of fresh, frozen or canned or one half cup of 100% pure juice. Alternatively, one cup of raw leafy vegetables or salads counts as a single serving, as well as a single piece of fruit (depending on its size). Keep pure juices to a minimum as they have a higher concentration of natural sugars and less fiber per serving, and this higher concentration of natural sugars also represents a higher concentration of calories.

The first and most important direction to lead you in, is to ensure that you are buying enough fruits and vegetables in the first place. Chances are if you don't have them available at your fingertips, you will miss many opportunities to introduce them into your diet: out of sight, out of mind. One helpful tip is to buy the recommended serving amounts for each member of your family for number of days you are shopping for. For example, if you are a family of four and shopping to get you through the next 3 days, you would need to buy a total of 84 servings of fruit and vegetables combined, based on an average of 7 servings each. Purchase these before proceeding to the other departments and aisles and build your meals based on these initial produce selections.

For example, an easy way to incorporate fresh spinach with every meal is to serve every piece of meat, chicken or fish on a bed of sautéed spinach leaves. Simply heat a pan over medium heat with a very small amount of olive oil, add a large handful of clean, fresh spinach leaves and season lightly with salt & pepper. They will cook and start to wilt very quickly as you toss with tongs. Plate immediately with your protein choice before they wilt too much, and serve right away.

If sandwiches are a meal item that you have regularly, then make sure you always have fresh lettuce, tomato and onions on hand at all times. Fresh spinach leaves are also great in a sandwich. A Mediterranean flair can also be added to your sandwiches by including roasted bell peppers or a spread of roasted fresh garlic.

Fruit can become an easily accessible snack item by always keeping containers of washed berries and grapes in your refrigerator at all times. Try not to pre-wash too much ahead of time however, as some fruits tend to deteriorate faster after washing. Always have a bowl of "grab & go" fruit and vegetables for those times when you're rushing out the door, like bananas, apples, mini-cucumbers, etc.

Vegetable skewers on the grill are another low fat and flavorful way to get your daily servings. Cold and wet weather days are not ideal conditions for firing up the grill but it does continue to offer low fat cooking year-round. If you can rearrange your grill's location to make it more easily accessible you will tend to use it more often. I have my barbecue undercover so I use it all the time.

Even if there is a member of your family that is somewhat fussy when it comes to eating fruits and vegetables, the produce departments seem to always be expanding in selection of imported/exotic goods. Buy something completely new for your family to try at least once per month. The Internet is filled with an abundance of information on preparing and serving almost any ingredient.

Another good habit to get into is to read the ingredient lists of premade prepackaged foods, if you are buying them. A recent trip to the grocery store to buy some "healthy" cereal revealed that there are a lot of choices that appear to be good for you, but really are not.

Upon reading the ingredient list it may be revealed that many are high in sugar. Even natural sugars, such as cane sugar, are still sugars and have many calories. One is better off buying rolled oats (not the instant variety) or 100% shredded wheat and adding some fresh fruit and low-fat milk. Obviously if you are used to eating high sugar cereals, these options may not taste as good at first. However, if you can find a way for your mind and taste buds to bask in the fact that you are eating much healthier, then this transition will be both literally and emotionally easier to swallow. Another way of approaching this, is to switch to unsweetened cereals, where you add your own sugar. Start by adding an amount of sugar that is satisfying and slowly wean to a smaller amount with the goal of eventually eliminating the added sugar altogether. This process of sugar elimination can also be done gradually with beverages such as coffee or tea… and if applicable, with cream too.

Again, have cream, but just not every day. And although having cream has no direct correlation to drinking red wine, I do feel compelled to state the following in my argument of moderation: I have read many studies suggesting that drinking a single glass of red wine every day is good for you, but skipping the whole week and having seven glasses on Friday... is not so good.

Butcher, Baker, Candlestick Maker

How well do you know your local butcher, baker, or candlestick maker? I realize that local candlestick makers are less prevalent than they use to be, but if you had one in your community they would be just as important as your other local merchants. We have all heard that shopping local is important to the economy and the environment, but do we know exactly why? The tentacles of this decision, to keep your money in the community spread out farther, and reap more benefits, than you can ever imagine.

I always make sure I get to know the people behind the counter on a first name basis. Not only for an opportunity to be friendly, but also to make sure I can get the best possible service. Saying hello and striking up conversations with proprietors and their employees every time I shop will help remind them about how often I am in their establishment spending money. Don't get me wrong, I love the personal aspect of making acquaintances and catching up with what's happening in their lives, and in the community, but I also want them to know how important

143

they are to me on a service level too. If they know I am frequenting the business they either own or work at, then they know I am contributing to the financial proceeds and the stability of that business. Because of this commitment on my part, they are more apt to go out of their way to get me what I may want or need in different circumstances. Spending money on products and services are transactions we will be doing for the rest of our lives, so we may as well gain additional rewards from where we spend each valued dollar. The friendships you make along the way will be an enriching bonus to your life.

Spending money at local businesses will keep more money in the communities we reside in. Firstly, this happens by maintaining the existing employment of their workers and, with growth, creating new jobs. Employment levels are always a key factor in the economic evaluations of any territory under scrutiny. Secondly, there is a good chance businesses employ people that reside in the same community. These employees, as well as the small business owners, are more likely to spend their money closer to home, than in other communities. We need to also consider what it takes for each of these small local businesses to operate; in other words, the services they purchase to keep their business functional. These services could include a local janitor or maintenance worker, local printing shop, and advertising/marketing services. It is more likely that a small business owner will use resources closer to home than large franchise stores.

In comparison to large big-box stores, small businesses tend to employ more people per unit of sale. Have you ever walked through a huge national chain store and found it difficult to locate someone to assist you? Their annual sales are massive, but yet per dollar, fewer people are needed to generate this income. This doesn't happen as much in small businesses. Not only will you be able to find someone more easily to assist you, but you are providing more jobs for every dollar you spend.

Another major impact that large national chain stores have made upon us, is the look of our neighborhoods. Have you ever traveled from city to city lately and notice that many areas are beginning to look identical? The same brand name stores are dotted everywhere, and many of them in very similar groupings. This has not only taken away from small businesses succeeding, but is also diminishing the uniqueness of each community. This in turn affects the local tourism industry as well. Disappearing are the unique looking shops and buildings, and the treasures you could possibly find inside.

For the most part, small businesses are more flexible at fulfilling our needs. They have the resources to provide the extra bit of service we may require, or the ability to bring in products that are out of the ordinary that we may desire. Large chain stores are more likely to be bound to contracts or procedures that keep their product offerings comparable. It is this reliability that keeps them popular among shoppers, but also can keep us from getting what we want. For example, where is the uniqueness of a gift for someone special if that product is offered in every community? Don't get me wrong, there are times when this dependability is beneficial to what we may be looking for, but we are missing out on tailoring these offerings to meet our needs. Take chain restaurants as another example. Many of them have a set menu, and staff trained on that menu, that they don't waiver from. Yes, they may have options or substitutions to cater to patrons that have dietary restrictions, but usually it is the small business eatery that will go out of their way to keep a customer coming back. This is mainly because each individual customer has a bigger impact on their small business. That same one customer in a business that pushes through hundreds or even thousands of customers each day, does not.

Another fact to consider when choosing to shop local is the impact on the environment. This is focusing on the source of the products being offered rather than the type of ownership of the business. The less distance these products have to travel before coming in contact with the end consumer, usually means the less harm to the environment because of reduced transportation and packaging needed. If products have to travel great distances (by means of trains, ships, trucks, etc.) before reaching a marketplace, the amount of emissions from these transportation sources increase dramatically compared to products that are sold at the source (like a local farm for example). We also need to keep in mind the additional and unnecessary use of nonrenewable resources as fuel for these transportation demands. Furthermore, less traveling means less chance of products being damaged, thus less packaging will be needed. Even if the packaging is recyclable, it still puts an added strain on the recycling resources more so than if it didn't have that additional packaging at all.

When considering fresh produce, one also should realize that many items are picked before they are fully ripe, so that they can ripen during transport. Fresh, direct, and fully ripe produce from the farm is always a better option for ultimate flavour and texture. Get in the habit of reading labels and asking questions about the origin of everything you purchase.

There is also a better chance that small local businesses will support fundraising and charities in the communities they are in. They are not bound to decision making rules set out by a corporate main office – they ARE the corporate office. Because they are connected with what's happening in the community, and the needs of the community, they are in a better position to adapt their charitable provisions more easily to help that cause.

With all of this said however, there is a cost factor that comes into play with the decision to support our local merchants. The relevant benefits must far outweigh the costs involved, but also we need to be able to literally afford the decision to shop local. If the budget for your household is holding your purse strings ransom, then you can only do what you can afford to do. Every argument I have given you here may make perfect sense, and it is not my intention to make you feel guilty if you cannot sustain these ideas one hundred percent. Awareness is my objective here. The more knowledgeable and aware we are, the better we can adapt our actions within our means. Get informed about the happenings and discussions in your communities. Search out social media pages that are dedicated to your area and follow (or start) discussions about where to shop and the products/services being offered. Please keep in mind that I am not suggesting that it always costs more to shop local; in fact, in many occasions, it may cost less. The more investigative work you do, the more mindful of this you will become. Every community, and the products/services being offered within, are different.

Another way to look at this, is to consider your household as a small business and become more mindful of the decisions you are making. Like a small business you have money coming in (income) and money going out (expenditures). Taking a closer look, and being conscious, of where and how your money is spent is never detrimental. Smart businesses always examine their financial statements, not only to see how successfully they are performing, but also to compare to previous years and situations. Perhaps there are some ways to reduce expenses in areas of your household to allow you to reevaluate the spending decisions you are currently making.

There are ways to expand your knowledge in the culinary world for example without negatively affecting your personal/family grocery budget. Let's face it, we all need to eat food to stay alive, and adding some variety to our home meals is a way to make "eating in" more exciting. How many times has the normal grocery shopping trip resulted in you bringing home the same old products that you always buy, for your stagnant home menu? This can very easily be changed without any drastic effect on your monthly food budget. Here's what I challenge you to do: every week, two weeks, or month, I want you to buy just one product you would never normally buy. This could be a produce item, a spice, a cheese you've never tried, etc. Take your blinders off, step outside your habitual boundaries, and be receptive to all the wonderful products we have available at our finger tips. No matter where you live, shopping today provides a greater opportunity for abundance of selection than ever before.

Talk to the local merchants selling the product and ask questions if you are unfamiliar with it and its uses or applications. The other great resource we have access to, whether at home, work or the local libraries, is the internet. This will allow you to answer questions about certain products that you have purchased that you may know nothing about. What do I do with it? How do I prepare it? How is it normally served? How is it best stored?

You and your family are going to be eating food anyway, and chances are you will continue to do so the rest of your life. What harm will it be then, to spend, for example, two or three dollars per month on one product you normally wouldn't purchase? Continue to do this for a year, while researching and educating yourself on each product and you will have expanded your culinary knowledge by twelve items. This will add variety to your home menu forever and at the same time build your culinary knowledge.

Many cities/towns also have gourmet food stores. Make it a habit to talk to these proprietors, tap into their expertise, and make your weekly/monthly one product purchase from their business instead of, or alternating with, your regular grocery store.

If you have even more room in your monthly budget, take a cooking class once per month instead of dining out. I know my restaurant friends will dislike me saying so, but the return on your investment in a cooking class is far greater than just a full stomach from one "dining out" visit. As the old saying goes "give a person a fish and you will feed them for a day; teach them to fish and you feed them for life".

Epilogue

Everyone has something they are passionate about. Think about that for a moment. We all have hobbies and pastimes that bring enjoyment to our lives; things we love doing and care tremendously about. These fascinations that we gravitate towards also keep many of our senses entertained. Take a moment to reflect on what some of your amusements may be.

One of mine for example, besides food and cooking, is old vehicles. It seems like I have always yearned for an old car to work on in the garage. This hobby ignites many of my senses: the sound of the engine roaring; the feel of getting behind the wheel; the sight of the distinct body lines and styles; I even love the unique scent of the musty cloth and vinyl interiors from days gone by. However, the one sense that is missing, and likely is from your hobbies too, that only comes through when eating or drinking, is taste.

Food and beverages not only rekindle that taste sense with every bite or sip, but also are vital to keeping us alive. It is that combination of sense exhilaration with nourishment for our bodies that make eating and drinking unique more so than anything else we do. And just as important, it is something that we all do. No matter what race or religion we are, what financial status or level of fame we have attained... we ultimately are all the same in this respect.

It is with that recognition, and comprehension, that we can enhance not only our own lives, but also the people around us. Who does not want to feel loved? Who would not welcome a kind, selfless gesture that would also nourish their body? I cannot think of a single soul.

Again, it is quite a statement to say that parsley, or rather food, is world peace in disguise, but it really is true. Imagine if our only focus on this earth was to welcome each other and to break bread together, what a different world this would be. All the dignitaries, the leaders of the countries, the people of power and monetary wealth, all coming together with any one, or all, of us just to share this one common denominator.

Embracing this theory, first and foremost, starts with you. Retrain yourself to love food again; to become blissfully lost in the colours, textures, aromas, sounds and tastes that encompasses this source of our survival. We are exposed to food and drink every single day of our lives and it is up to us to choose to not only recognize its impact, but embrace it as well. We are given the gift the to make choices in everything we do, and many times shifting our focus is all we need to do to see the good in something.

Be proud of who you are and the life you have been blessed with. Respect and honor other people that are living similar journeys to yours, and find opportunities to bring joy and happiness to their lives, as you would enjoy the same if directed towards you.

Nothing is out of reach. It is only unattainable if you choose it to be. Everything starts with an idea... which creates an opening... then begins new habits, and ultimately new results.

Footnotes: Page about the definition of chore in "Cooking is Not Vacuuming" chapter

i Webster's New World College Dictionary
http://www.yourdictionary.com/chore#websters (accessed January7, 2017)

Katherine (Mrs. Dez) and Chef Dez

ABOUT THE AUTHOR

Chef Dez (Gordon Desormeaux) resides in the Fraser Valley of British Columbia, Canada with his family. His passion for food and people is second to none and anyone who has attended his live performances would agree. Thousands of have rekindled their romance for the culinary arts because of his infectious enthusiasm for bringing ingredients together.

Also the Author of
The Best In Your Kitchen
and other great cookbooks

www.chefdez.com

Made in the USA
San Bernardino, CA
05 September 2017